Praise for *The Hunt*

"David Farbman's *The Hunt* teaches you how to tap into your own inner hunter to find the killer clarity that you need to aim with pinpoint accuracy at your most meaningful goals in life."

> —**Dan Gilbert,** founder and chairman,
> Quicken Loans Inc.

"By utilizing David Farbman's principles in *The Hunt*, not only have I significantly grown Carbon Media Group but I've made meaningful improvements in my personal life."

> —**Hyaat Chaudhary,** CEO,
> Carbon Media Group

"*The Hunt* is on target. David has taken the basic principles of hunting and used them to create a focused playbook for success in business or personal life. A killer read for any business or outdoor enthusiast. It helped us tremendously at the office and in our personal lives."

> —**Mike and Stacey Marsh,** founders,
> Flatout Bread

"*The Hunt* takes you on a wild ride from the backwoods to the boardroom. You will never look at business or life in the same way after you read this book."

> —**Kim Brink,** VP, marketing, NASCAR

"The way *The Hunt* ties together the outdoors, business, and life is really cool."
> **—Michael Waddell,** star, *Michael Waddell's Bone Collector*

"*The Hunt* provides an easily applicable way of accomplishing the goals that have otherwise eluded you."
> **—Heather Stewart,** national advertising manager, Chevy Trucks

"*The Hunt* is awesome and can help every generation."
> **—Rob Goldman,** director of product management, Facebook

The
HUNT

TARGET, TRACK, AND ATTAIN YOUR GOALS

DAVID FARBMAN

JB JOSSEY-BASS™
A Wiley Brand

Published by Jossey-Bass
A Wiley Brand
One Montgomery Street, Suite 1200, San Francisco, CA 94104-4594
www.josseybass.com

Jossey-Bass books and products are available through most bookstores. To contact Jossey-Bass directly call our Customer Care Department within the U.S. at 800-956-7739, outside the U.S. at 317-572-3986, or fax 317-572-4002.

Wiley publishes in a variety of print and electronic formats and by print-on-demand. Some material included with standard print versions of this book may not be included in e-books or in print-on-demand. If this book refers to media such as a CD or DVD that is not included in the version you purchased, you may download this material at **http://booksupport.wiley.com.** For more information about Wiley products, visit **www.wiley.com.**

Library of Congress Cataloging-in-Publication Data

Library of Congress Cataloging-in-Publication Data has been applied for and is on file with the Library of Congress.

ISBN 978-1-118-85824-0 (cloth); ISBN 978-1-118-88630-4 (ePDF);
ISBN 978-1-118-88645-8 (ePub)

Printed in the United States of America

FIRST EDITION

HB Printing   10 9 8 7 6 5 4 3 2 1

To the outdoors and all who love it,
and to my amazing family for supporting me
through endless hours spent building companies,
creating The Hunt Platform, and being one with nature

CONTENTS

Hunter, Gatherer, CEO? An Introduction to
The Hunt   1

1   Getting Up, Getting Clear: Consciousness   15

2   Keeping it Real: Authenticity   51

3   Taking Trophies: Leverage   95

4   Bringing it Home: Real-Time Execution   143

5   Finding Flow and Leaving a Clean Wake   183

NOTES   201

ACKNOWLEDGMENTS   205

ABOUT THE AUTHOR   209

INDEX   211

The
HUNT

HUNTER, GATHERER, CEO? AN INTRODUCTION TO *THE HUNT*

Do you consider yourself a hunter?

Your answer should be "yes." In fact, even if you've never held a gun or a bow, don't believe in killing, rarely get out into the woods or on the water, you're just the hunter I'm looking for. Have you ever dated, played sports, or held a job? Have you ever bought a car? Gone after a promotion? Sold an idea? Yes, that's all hunting. We humans are *always* hunting—trying to track down and take the things we want, the things that will make our life bigger, better, safer; more satisfying, exciting, and just plain *fun*. We're at the top of the food chain, which makes us super-predators, and hunting is simply in our nature.

Most people seem to have forgotten how powerful nature can be. In fact, the older we get, the more time most of us human beings spend trying to muzzle our natural instincts, instead of leveraging them to find and take opportunity. And I do mean "take," not "make." A lot of

B-school sages and motivational gurus earn money by telling people over and over again that they have to go out and "create opportunity." But that's not how alphas rise to the top of their pack. The most successful hunters of any species know that *life* creates opportunity—that all of the elements for any version of success we can imagine are already in our territory, thanks to the constant flow of experience, circumstance, interaction, observation, innovation, evolution, and revolution that surrounds us.

Like successful hunters in all species, our challenge is to identify every opportunity in our environment and then leverage those that can best advance us toward our ultimate goals. When we have absolute clarity about who we are and an unwavering focus on what we want to achieve, we can build momentum within that flow of opportunity, of life, overtaking the Desired Outcomes we've targeted, then anticipating, identifying, and closing in on fresh targets on the horizon. That's The Hunt in action. It's how wild predators rule their territory and how we, as True Hunters, can achieve results in our own hunt for success, no matter how you define that term.

Of course, I'm not the only one out there leveraging hunting skills in business, the arts, education, and government; all great decision makers, humanitarians, and business leaders use the tactics of The Hunt method. I'm just clearing the trail, opening up the canopy to bring in daylight, placing key markers and guideposts along the path. This book will offer the insights I've taken from my biggest scores—and misfires—as an entrepreneur, CEO, innovator, disruptive thinker, husband, father, and lifelong hunter. And it will introduce you to a pack of other business and social leaders who have used their human nature and primal skills to take the alpha slot and command any territory in which they've chosen to hunt.

For example, we'll meet Quicken Loans CEO and founder Dan Gilbert, who used his skills as a True Hunter to develop a technology and marketing machine that has enabled him to blaze new trails in business and philanthropy. I'll introduce you to some fellow True Hunters who called themselves the Bone Collector Brotherhood: three guys who turned their passion for hunting into a national television phenomenon. We'll track down the success of Kim Brink, who has used her unique brand of Authenticity to become a trailblazing marketing pro with some of the world's most successful companies. The experiences you'll read about in these profiles—along with the lessons I learned while targeting wins in Michigan's woods, Manhattan boardrooms, and the lobbying bullpens of Washington, DC—will offer you a powerful arsenal of weapons for tracking down and claiming your own trophies in the hunt for success.

I began The Hunt at an early age; my parents taught me how to fish and hunt when I was nine years old. I was a hyper, talkative, highly social and energetic kid. My dad's gut told him that the quiet, targeted process of tracking animals and observing their behavior would help focus my attention and calm me down. And he was right. Spending time in the outdoors, learning to "read" my environment, observing and tracking animals, all helped me get in touch with my human nature and develop my senses and primal skills in a way most people never realize. I learned how to *really* see the world, to make decisions and approach problems in a way that kept me centered, tightly focused, and very aware. I learned to disregard my ego and ignore the distractions of false leads and cold trails. Hunting taught me to set my sights on a target and then use every available skill, technique, experience, and opportunity to go after and get it. Over the years, I honed the abilities I needed to become an entrepreneur, leader, decision maker, problem solver, and a decent human being—a True Hunter.

The principles, tactics, and lessons of hunting became my blueprint for life. I used them to build businesses that triumphed over some pretty experienced competitors. I learned patience, strategy, stealth, execution, and adaptability. I became more authentic, completely comfortable in my own skin and willing to help others shed their own camouflage. Best of all, I'm happy. I've launched a number of successful companies that own their markets by being high-energy engines of innovation—fun places to work, staffed with a diverse crowd of very cool, creative, outcome-driven people. Beyond financial rewards, I'm even richer in family and friends and long-term professional allies. These people are always ready to wade into a new venture with me, watch my back, and take a shot at bigger, bolder, and more exciting targets. I still make mistakes, as every hunter does. But I've learned that this tends to happen when I go off-trail, become foggy about the target I'm pursuing, or stray from the principles of hunting and life that I've learned over the years.

The Hunt is about becoming the most successful hunter you can be. It will teach you how crucial it is to own your nature, lead with authenticity, and identify and pursue your goals using powerful natural instincts and primal skills. *The Hunt* method opens your eyes and mind to a world of more pleasure, satisfaction, security, creativity, innovation, influence, and financial scores—in other words, a world that delivers greater personal and professional success, whatever your definition of the term. I built a cutting-edge online enterprise on the principles of hunting, so I know how relevant this approach is in today's technology-obsessed world. In fact, I don't think there's ever been a *better* time to leverage the tools and techniques in *The Hunt*.

A Guide to *The Hunt*

One of the first things I learned as a young hunter was that there's a lot of freedom in just a little structure. To give you the clearest path through The Hunt method and the most freedom in deciding how to make that journey, I've structured its ideas, processes, and practices into five major pillars—the elements of The Hunt that we'll tackle in this book:

- **Consciousness:** True Hunters know how to be present, in the moment, alive and aware. They rise above the noise and clutter of their ego, the constant demands on their attention, and the occasionally crazy events taking place around them. They're able to observe the world as a Scout, not a Judge—terms I introduce in Chapter One. I also lay out some specific practices and techniques you can use to develop your own hunter's *consciousness* and to sharpen your senses, train your focus, and deepen your understanding of people and events. That kind of clarity will allow you to predict developments and stay on track, even when aiming at fast-moving targets. In fact, I'll show you how to slow those targets down and make your shot when the one best moment presents itself.

- **Authenticity:** You can't fake your way to sustainable success in *any* area of life. Being real—up-front and honest about your motives, Desired Outcomes, capabilities, and needs—is one of the most powerful advantages you can take with you into any hunt. In Chapter Two, I offer specific tools for using a hunter's *authenticity* to see yourself and your goals with sharp clarity, disarm your opponents, select key strategic partners, and develop powerful alliances. The ideas and techniques you'll learn here will help you embrace the authenticity that allows you to walk with confidence down the trail ahead.

- **Leverage:** True Hunters are the ultimate opportunists—the most successful people in any area of business and life. They use every sensory data point, every element of past experience, every person, tool, weapon, and event they encounter to achieve their goals. And they expect to *give* the same kind of *leverage* points to others. Think of the key processes you learn in Chapter Three as weight-training for your "leverage muscle." With practice, using leverage will become as natural as breathing—your reflexive response in any situation, allowing you to move beyond small targets and take the trophies that deserve space on your walls.

- **Real-Time Execution:** Ideas and energy matter, but when it comes to hunting successfully, *execution* rules. Real-time execution requires that you hone in on a desired outcome and then target your ongoing decisions and actions to achieve the win—even in a fast-moving and ever-changing environment. In Chapter Four, I describe an arsenal of tools and practices you can use to focus on prime targets, develop key strategies for taking them, tune your tactical approach on the fly, and continually adjust the trajectory of your short-term goals so that you are constantly advancing in the overall direction you've chosen for your work and your life. You'll leave this chapter of *The Hunt* with solid methods for focusing on solutions, staying on track, knowing when to pivot, identifying breakthrough moments in your progress, and celebrating the breakout moments you've been hunting for.

- **Flow:** When you see the world around you clearly—when you know who you are and what you want, own your Desired Outcomes, and commit to doing whatever it takes to claim them—you naturally align yourself with the people, places, events, and ideas that surround and support that outcome. This kind of alignment is my version of *flow*—a concept of concentrated, inspired performance that modern-day psychologists and ancient eastern religions have described and that the world's most successful hunters demonstrate, from the jungle of venture capitalism to the plains of the African veldt. In Chapter Five, I describe the process of harnessing the power of flow. You'll learn how flow powers you toward the successes you've set your sights on and how it keeps you at the top of your game as a True Hunter—always on track toward bigger and better outcomes and as committed to the legacy you'll leave behind as you are to carving out the road ahead.

I can't predict what lies ahead on the path *The Hunt* will open up for you. But I *can* guarantee that this method will set you on the trail of some of the most important quests of your life.

How *The Hunt* Took Shape

Even the most successful hunter wanders off course now and then. It's actually the process of making and recovering from mistakes that supplies one of our most valuable learning tools. That's the lesson I took away from a painful misstep that landed me squarely in the cross-hairs of some of the most ferocious opponents I've ever faced. The journey I made into and then out of that disaster gave me a whole new perspective on the way my primal instincts and lifelong experience as a hunter have helped shape my approach to business, relationships, and life itself—an understanding that formed the foundation for *The Hunt.*

That journey began in 2006, when I began pursuing a goal I'd first imagined ten years earlier: a televised, no-kill, pro hunting tour called the World Hunting Association (WHA), which would showcase the methods that professional hunters use to read their environment and track their prey. I had been looking for a way to bring hunting into the mainstream consciousness, to highlight its role as a way to understand other species and connect with nature. By using a tranquilizer instead of a bullet or a fatal broadhead, the stigma of the killing off the table, the idea seemed like a no-brainer to me. And, unfortunately, a "no-brainer" is exactly what it turned out to be.

I powered through with passion, convinced that I was heading toward something huge—maybe even the NASCAR of hunting. But when the hunting industry got wind of the tournament's nonfatal spin, I went from the fast-track launch of a revolutionary new outdoor event to a desperate fight for professional survival. Suddenly I was the target of a national online "kill" campaign launched by industry lobbyists who are represented in Washington DC. As the campaign went viral, my WHA sponsors and the hunting organizations and groups I'd been part of for years turned on me. My reputation as a businessman, decision maker, and sportsman was dying before my eyes—and that was just the first leg of the adventure.

The pain of that fall drove me back to the place where the whole thing had started—in nature, on the trail of a white-tailed deer, at home with the place, purpose, and skills I knew best. On a clear autumn day, I fled the storm and headed to my family's farm in Michigan. As I walked into the woods, my ego finally shut up and I felt calm for the first time in weeks. I climbed into the highest tree stand on the property and sat for hours trying to see my situation from a clear perspective. Eventually, my True Hunter's consciousness took over. It allowed me to see the goal I'd been pursuing, where I'd lost sight of my target, and what I had to do to get back on the trail of the original outcome I'd set out to capture.

During the two gut-wrenching years that followed, I used every skill, principle, and tactic I'd learned in nature to fight my way back. I used past career successes and experiences to face the leadership challenges before me. I leveraged every opportunity I could to pivot my business model. The result was OutdoorHub, a business that soon owned its marketplace as the world's largest online showcase for outdoor enthusiast media.

The experience of turning my failure with the WHA into the foundation for an even bigger targeted outcome convinced me that I was armed to take what I needed in any territory or market. A lifetime of hunting had made me relentlessly committed to winning, but it had also given me the strategic mind-set and tactical skills I needed to go out and make that win happen. And that's the approach to capturing success—in business and in life—that I map out in the following pages.

Where Will *The Hunt* Take You?

For years, I've shared my approach with friends, colleagues, and clients from a wide variety of disciplines and interests, and I haven't been at all surprised at how well it works. The reason for that success is simple. Rather than driving people to become something they're not, The

Hunt method simply helps people maximize the talents they were born with. As the True Hunter in you takes the lead, you naturally shift into a new way of thinking about yourself and the world you live in and what possibilities life offers.

The Hunt is all about developing your instincts, skills, and natural competitive advantages. It shows you how to practice the discipline of cool, egoless assessment and action, expand your consciousness and awareness, feel comfortable in your own skin, and eliminate the distractions of pointless insecurity and false priorities in order to observe without judging and act without fear. Adopting the calm and centered approach of a True Hunter will allow you to

- Get a bigger, clearer picture of your life and goals, and discover things about yourself and your ability that you've never noticed or seen before
- Learn to attract more dynamic people, generate more positive energy and results, and build a more fulfilling life
- Change your attitudes and outcomes so that you enjoy more productive hunts and can target your mindset and actions on getting the trophies you're *really* aiming for
- Treat conversations and other moments of your life far more consciously and deeply in order to obtain those outcomes

- Overcome obstacles by focusing on macro issues of solutions, not the micro level of problems
- Harness and leverage every opportunity to obtain your Desired Outcomes and inspire your best thinking

Perhaps most important of all, the principles of *The Hunt* give you a clearer, sharper lens for seeing the world and shaping your role in it. You'll make better decisions, form stronger alliances, build better strategies, target bigger wins, and uncover more opportunities. Best of all, you will face life as a True Hunter—someone who knows who they are, what they want, and how to get what they're hunting for. You'll leave *The Hunt* with the ability to identify and leverage opportunities at a whole new level, to see every challenge you face in a clearer, more authentic light—to have more control over your actions and outcomes than you've ever had before.

If you are 100 percent content with your life and don't want to challenge your beliefs or go against the grain of conventional wisdom, then this book isn't for you. If you never question your path forward, wander into a blind alley, or struggle through messy business decisions, personal relationships, or any of life's other common minefields, then this book probably won't feel very useful to you. (In fact, what are you doing here, anyway? You should be taking *me* on a hunt!)

However, if you came onto this earth as a curious and engaged human being—if you're pretty certain that you don't know everything and you might really benefit from developing the focus, vision, and disciplined tracking skills of a True Hunter—then you're in for an incredible ride. I'm about to take you up into the tree stand and then down the trail. We're going to hit the woods together and go get what we're looking for, because around here, success is always in season.

The Hunt is on.

GETTING UP, GETTING CLEAR: CONSCIOUSNESS

I once spent nearly three years hunting a deer I named Elvis. He was a savvy old buck who owned the woods on Timber Ridge Ranch, the northern Michigan property I've been blessed to hunt on for the better part of my life. Elvis truly was "the King"; the spread of massive antlers and the incredible bulk of his body put him in a different class from every other buck on the ranch. He and I crossed paths on several occasions, and I drew my bow once, but he never presented me with a clear shot. I can still remember every time he got away from me, and I'd like to say that he escaped my arrows through twists of fate and dumb luck. But the truth is, that bad boy outsmarted me. He was as familiar with his territory as he was with his heartbeat; he knew where he needed to go to eat, mate, and rest, and he knew the best ways to get there. His senses were on fire, so he didn't miss any sight, sound, or smell in the woods around him, and he knew *precisely* how to respond to any potential danger (like me) that he might face. And while he did get lucky now and then, it was his own doing. As my mom would say, "Luck is at the side of the able navigator."

My parents unlocked the door to a whole new world for me when they taught me to hunt and fish, and lessons like "the able navigator" were the key. Great hunters have to be great navigators, concerned with a whole lot more than just dodging hazards and getting around the next turn. They must imagine the entire journey they're undertaking from the very beginning. They can't plan that journey at ground level, or just plow ahead and "see what happens"; they have to form a big-picture understanding of the territory they're traversing, and it must account for every data point that stands between them and their destination. That's how they're able to map out the safest, most direct route and find the best alternatives for pivoting around hazards and roadblocks that crop up along the way.

It took some time for me to really get Mom's message. But I now know from experience that the people who have the most luck are the ones who do the best job of seeing the world around them through a panoramic lens. With that perspective, they can prepare to make the most of whatever comes their way. As a True Hunter, you'll have luck along the way. But, just like any able navigator, you set yourself up to *be* lucky. You won't have to hope for miracles if things start to go south.

True Hunters know that you have to look high before you look low when you're in The Hunt. You can't just hit the ground and start hacking your way through the undergrowth or follow every animal path or distant noise you hear in search of a trophy white-tail, and you can't let yourself be distracted by clashing egos and false alarms when you're tracking down critical issues in a tangled business environment. You'll waste all sorts of time chasing after shadows; and in the process, you'll drive away the game you're really after. Instead, you have to climb up into the tree stand; get above all of the noise and clutter of ego, assumptions, and conflict; and position yourself to gather as many data points as possible. Then you can get quiet, concentrate, and let all of your senses work together to form a much broader and deeper understanding of the territory in which you're hunting. You can plot out the best path forward, toward your target. You're present, aware, and alert to the world around you. That's *consciousness:* the first element of The Hunt method, and the most fundamental skill set you'll rely on in any pursuit.

In The Hunt, consciousness is a state of panoramic understanding in which your mind is neutral and your vision remains focused, no matter how crazy the action around you becomes. Your ego keeps its mouth shut and gives you the mental clarity you need to listen, observe, and assess. You feel steady and in control, even when that massive buck—or monster deal or irate client—is right in front of you. You can see far more from this elevated perspective than you can when you're tangled in conflicting agendas or caught in the ego traps of shame or fear. Remaining above all of these allows you to scout out the clearest pathway through the false leads, brambles, predators, and pitfalls and on toward your short-term targets, your Desired Outcomes (DO), and your ultimate goals.

Climbing into the Tree Stand

Don't tell me you've never fallen into this trap, because it gets us all at some point: You're desperate to find a solution to a burning issue *fast*. Your mind races over one idea after another until you finally see a small glimmer of hope way out on the horizon. Instead of pulling that idea into a big-picture understanding, collecting all relevant data points, exploring possible consequences, you decide to just *go for it*. You dive in, bust your butt clearing a path for each step forward, and then you hit a wall—then another—and eventually you realize you're going in circles and have no viable way to move ahead. Now you're trapped. Your ignorance has driven you straight into the jaws of fear.

Fear is the deadliest trap for any hunter, because it blocks your ability to see everything that's going on around you. It keeps you from being able to assess the dangers you face and determining your chances for taking them out. Your world becomes narrower, the trap becomes tighter, and you can react only with more fear, more panic, more blind thrashing around.

Even experienced hunters have been known to "shoot before they hunt"—running blindly through unscouted territory, taking potshots at something they haven't really seen. That's exactly the mistake I made when I allowed my ego to guide me in launching the World Hunting Association (WHA). I was so worried about someone snatching my idea that I didn't bother discussing the no-kill angle of the tournament with *any* industry contacts. Instead of looking at the tournament from their—my target's—perspective, anticipating the blowback, and defusing it before it occurred, I just plowed on. I assumed my idea was so wildly out-of-the-box successful that everything would "just work out." I was wrong—and totally unprepared to deal with the backlash. So I know how easy it is to be blinded by ego and then stumble into the jaws of fear. But that experience taught me that when you feel yourself getting sucked into that trap, running in circles or freezing in panic won't save you.

Instead, you need to climb up into the tree stand above your ego and outside your own mind to start assessing your situation from a neutral perspective. From there, you can take a calm, clear look at yourself and the challenges and opportunities you're facing. Acting with consciousness means being guided by reality, not driven by fear. It allows you to keep an objective mind and stay keenly focused on your target, your DO.

Climbing into the elevated viewpoint of consciousness takes some practice. However, it's an essential first step for navigating your way through any quicksand or pitfall that lies between you and your DO. Learning a few critical skills and the disciplined practice of consciousness is where that hunt begins. The following short exercise is a great starting point in that work. You can use it to get comfortable with the idea of eyeing a challenge or opportunity from this perspective:

1. Find a relatively quiet place where you can spend fifteen minutes or so in uninterrupted silence—no phone, email, or other intrusions.
2. Take three deep breaths; as you're doing that, visualize a large tree standing before you.
3. Let your mind's eye move up the tree, above your body, to where you can look down and see your position and everything surrounding it in one panoramic view.
4. Now, as the Scout, look around the "you" that is left on the ground and note the details of the situation that surrounds that image—the people, the events taking place, the physical landscape.
5. Find the target you want to hit, the place you want to go—your DO. What can you see that separates you from it? How tough are these obstacles? Which ones can you knock down? Which should you try to change? And which should you bypass as quietly as possible?

Every step of The Hunt should be focused on *out-comes*. That's why it's crucial to train yourself to climb high enough to spot and clearly see those outcomes. This is how you'll identify the key *and* the driver for every move you make. When you're in the consciousness "zone," you're better able to understand just what end result you really want to arrive at. Are you gunning for more money? A promotion? Stronger business partners? A better relationship with your spouse or kids? A more meaningful direction for your life? Hunting with consciousness allows you to see everything in your world more clearly—people, ideas, events, emerging trends, and the connections that link them all together. That perspective brings into focus the long-term outcomes you desire, and the short-term goals you'll need to take down in order to hit them.

Learning to get above your ego will teach you to see the world as it is: clearly, completely, with no blind spots or camouflage. It puts you in a near-meditative state; active, alert, calm, but fully hooked in to your surroundings. This kind of "getting high" actually grounds you in a reality that's bigger than any single problem you may be facing. You'll see the world as predator *and* prey, and use that killer clarity to visualize the entire hunt before you. Eventually, you'll be able to make this climb in any situation—even in the midst of important conversations, critical meetings, or other highly charged events. But start with this first, basic visual work on your own.

It will help you get used to pushing egos and other "clutter" out of the way, so you can make a careful, comprehensive observation about the issues, opportunities, and obstacles you're *really* facing. Over time, you'll find that getting into that elevated viewpoint is as natural to you as breathing, as consciousness becomes the first step in your go-to approach to problem solving, decision making, and leadership.

Being There: The Scout and the Judge

Your next step in the journey toward consciousness is learning to show up in your life, to truly *be there*—alive, awake, and totally engaged with the territory around you. When you're really present, you are a *Scout*, not a *Judge*. You're able to observe yourself and the events taking place around you without filtering the view through your ego or allowing the Judge to drag you into the jaws of insecurity and fear. While we each have our own version, the Judge's droning voice sounds something like this:

"Stop looking confused! And don't give in—you always give in. Aw, no! You forgot your smartphone, so you can't check that schedule. What an idiot. Look at Paul—he's an idiot, too, but you know he's going to try to shut you down on your proposal. Why is he such a jerk? Why didn't you spend more time prepping on interim deliverables? Why are you always the last one to figure this stuff out? Damn, you should have applied for that job in Jersey. What would you do if you

lost this gig? You've got to make this job work—it's probably the best you can get."

That's the Judge talking—and talking and *talking*. Once you let him get started, it can be unbelievably hard to shut him up. In fact, if you listen long enough, you simply *become* the Judge, and his negative self-talking controls everything you do.

The voice of the Judge is nothing more than our ego messing with us. The fear it evokes may feel real, but it *isn't*—unless we choose to give it life by listening. So, if you want to be absolutely certain that you'll lose money in a deal, then start saying to yourself, "I won't be able to pull this thing off. Too late to do anything about it now. It's gonna fail, and when it does, I'm screwed." And guess what? You'll be right! All you have to do is keep listening, and all of those bad predictions *will come true.*

The Judge specializes in sidetracking you *just* when you most need to stay on target. Worse, his damaging self-talk becomes an excuse for failure. Instead of elevating your perspective, the Judge drags you down to where you lose *all* perspective, *all* clarity on your DO and the people and events that surround it. But when you focus your thoughts and actions intensely on a *positive* target, you're in a position to start tracking it.

If the Judge rules your brain every time you find yourself in a tough spot, I have an important piece of advice: step away from the center of the universe! Believe me,

I get it. We learn self-absorbed, ego-driven routines almost from birth. This makes it all the more difficult to silence the Judge's harsh reminders of our fears and shortcomings. But *you* are not the focal point in every challenge you face—your *target*, your *goal* is the point. And the Judge's nonstop trash talk can make it easy to lose track of that important reality.

If you're going in circles instead of progressing toward your goal, the Judge is taking control. So just stop—and then follow this simple, three-step exercise:

1. **Take a quick time-out to determine exactly what you're feeling.** Are you afraid? Do you feel anxious? Is your stress building? Are you listening to your fear, instead of focusing like a laser on the words, actions, and events going down around you? Try to identify ego-driven distractions like these that might be cluttering your path forward. Now ask yourself: How is this serving me?

2. **Take yourself out of the picture, and focus on your Desired Outcome.** Step back, climb up above your ego, and observe the big picture, *always* with your focus trained on how every element within it relates to your DO. Ask yourself: What do I want? What's standing in my way? What first forward steps can I take? List all of your answers on paper; you can even sketch them out as a graph to give yourself a visual guide to the process ahead (more about the process of identifying DOs in just a bit).

3. **Take action.** Listening to the Judge will trap you in fear, but action will free you. Don't worry about making a wrong move. Just make some sort of move, and let that lead you to the next. The path ahead may bend here and there, but your focus needs to remain fixed on your target—your DO—and every move you make should advance you toward that goal. But you need to take that first step.

With this process, you've flipped from Judge to Scout. You can observe the big picture, be present, and return your focus to the reality of *now*. You're operating with a neutral mind, collecting data points, identifying obstacles, weighing options, and preparing yourself for a successful hunt—no matter where it may take you.

You don't have to wait for a crisis to practice the discipline of consciousness. You can use this exercise and other techniques outlined in this chapter to develop your clarity and awareness all day, every day. For example: instead of worrying about screwing up a presentation or plotting some vigilante justice for that jerk who cut you off when you were driving to work, tune out the Judge and put the Scout to work. Focus on the big picture—what you want to accomplish with that presentation and how your plan will get you there; what clues to next moves you can pick up from the drivers around you; and what leverage points that information gives you for making your own drive as painless as possible.

As the Scout, you're living in the real world, not fighting dragons in your mind. You want your presentation to kill, you want to get to work without having a wreck, and you want to deal with *everyone* as successfully as possible. The real world is always out there, feeding you information, delivering data points that can bring you critical ammunition for hitting your targets and taking the trophies. You just have to be there to take it all in.

Checking into Rehab

Few things are more depressing and nonproductive than our ego's nagging voice. So why do we listen to it? Well, it's a habit, and one that I believe has both physical and emotional triggers—sort of like a drug addiction. Our brains guide our actions by building synapses and firing neurons that tell us how to respond to the world around us. When we rehearse the same kinds of negative thoughts over and over again, our brains learn that destructive pattern—and our actions conform to it. We're at risk of making what was just a worry—a negative fantasy—into a negative reality, a world where we expect the worst, and we *get* the worst.

That's a habit you have to break. Think of consciousness and the combined elements of The Hunt method as rehab, the detox you need to purge the Judge's negative garbage from your thoughts and beliefs.

When you move into a state of consciousness, it's easier to lose the Judge's negative influence on your life.

But be aware that he's still going to be in charge of a lot of the people around you—so be careful not to fall back into old patterns. Spend as little time as possible with others who are under the control of negativity. You don't want to be lured back to that dark space. Use your consciousness to be alert to *all* of the influences that cross your path, so that you can see them for what they are and keep moving forward—no sidetracks, no dead ends, no downward spirals.

Sighting the Target: Desired Outcomes

Without a designated target for your hunt, you're going nowhere. And *really* understanding what it is you're shooting for isn't quite as easy as it might seem. I've spent a lifetime learning to spot whitetails in the forest, so I can tell you that it's a lot easier to see a well-camouflaged deer in a thicket than it is to identify an undefined outcome hiding behind a cluster of fuzzy half-formed goals. That's why identifying the Desired Outcome that you're aiming for is an important step in developing consciousness and the absolute clarity it provides.

Identifying your Desired Outcome, your DO, is a tricky business. That's because most of us grow up learning to ignore our real desires or to hide them behind something bigger, sexier, or more socially acceptable—which is a great way to *never* hit your target. And many of our targets are tangled up in our egos and identity, making them incredibly difficult to see or understand (we talk more about the authenticity of our DOs in Chapter Two). Most people have to *deliberately practice* slowing down at this stage of consciousness, so they can strip away the camouflage, identify what they *really* want out of any situation, and then take the next step toward claiming it.

Your first step in making that ID is to ask yourself two simple questions:

1. What do you want?
2. Why do you want it?

I ask those questions of myself and of anyone who comes to me for advice about gritty issues like resolving a conflict at work, closing a deal, or dealing with a downwardly spiraling relationship. They're straightforward questions; if you can't answer them, you have virtually zero chance of resolving things to *anyone's* satisfaction.

Most DOs move us forward when we find solutions to problems or eliminate their source. But getting at those root problems or issues can take some thought. The word "root" is the key, because you have to be able to cut to the very source of the challenge in order to understand what you're truly hunting for. Of course, when you've answered question 1, and you have a pretty clear idea of what goal you're targeting, you still have to deal with question 2—*why* are you targeting it? To flush that answer out of hiding, you may have to ask yourself some other questions:

- If I get this Desired Outcome, what does that success look like?
- What does solving this problem bring me?
- How will the outcome feel?
- Will I have moved forward? Or will I have just moved sideways, or even backward, in relationship to the bigger outcomes and goals I've set for myself?

Be *very clear* when you answer these questions. Life is constantly changing, so your goals will always be somewhat fluid. But you need to be able to measure a solid DO in some way—as this is the only way to know with absolute clarity whether or not you've achieved it.

Taking time to think through what you want, why you want it, and how you might feel when you get it is an important step in hunting with consciousness. If you can't be completely clear about your Desired Outcome, you won't be able to form a solid plan for taking it down, and you sure won't be able to defend your plan or lead others in the hunt to accomplish it. Your crystal clear visualization of your DO forms the target *and* the trophy that you and your allies will pursue. And developing the right Desired Outcome helps keep everyone's ego at bay. It only takes one "me, Me, ME!" spin-out in a meeting to tank the chances for a productive resolution. I have seen countless projects with massive potential tank because someone's ego got out of check—and the group lost focus on its desired endpoint. If we know exactly what we want and remain committed to obtaining it, we're in a better position to keep even the biggest egos subordinated to that overriding goal.

The person in the room who can be grounded and present—who can help keep the group focused on a clear vision of the Desired Outcome—will always emerge as the True Hunter in any organization. I want this person to be you. When others see you as the one who can hang steady when the pressure is on, everyone else will be ready to back you when situations heat up. And you can pretty much count on the fact that things will get heated from time to time. Tracking down dangerous game isn't a bad thing. In fact, the more skillful you become as a True Hunter, the more passion and joy you'll find in achieving oversized wins or stopping unpredictable, rapidly moving problems dead in their tracks. We need to take on tougher challenges if we want to keep growing and flowing, and your skills of consciousness help keep you on track to achieve your Desired Outcomes, no matter how much weight they drag along with them.

Dan Gilbert: Master of Clarity

You won't find a hunter with a more targeted focus on Desired Outcomes than Dan Gilbert. Dan is the founder and chairman of Quicken Loans, a company that handles more direct-to-consumer home mortgage loans than any other organization in the world. He also is the majority owner in a number of professional sport teams and chairman of Rock Gaming, the company that is opening Horseshoe Casinos throughout the Midwest. Dan's a True Hunter, and the clear view of consciousness rules his game. "Clarity is a big word around here," he told me. And for Dan, defining a Desired Outcome is central to reaching that place of clarity: "So much of the world is vague and muddy. I don't even want to meet with people who can't tell me what they want to get out of the meeting."

Dan's had plenty of practice in learning to define and pursue his own Desired Outcomes over the years. Growing his fledgling loan business was a difficult hunt—for big game. He knew that he had to scale the business, but how could he possibly pull in the number of people and build the number of locations he'd need to occupy a real presence in the national marketplace? "The process of closing a home loan is a killer," he explained. "We closed 42,000 loans last month. As crazy as it sounds, when we closed 420 loans a month, it was a lot harder. It was loan-to-loan combat. I couldn't keep up."

Back then, Gilbert struggled with the idea of growing his staff and infrastructure to handle the bulky and time-consuming loan process. But when Gilbert got up above all of that noise and studied the issue from a broader perspective, he was able to identify the solution. He didn't need to figure out how to *do more* of what he was doing; he needed to find a better, more scalable way of doing loans— period. As Gilbert explains: "It came to me that all lending is local. I realized that I had to come up with a system—the technology, the process—to close loans in fifty states, two thousand counties, from a centralized environment. If we could do that, I knew we'd go big."

While Gilbert was able to clearly identify his Desired Outcome, he still had a lot of work to do—and a big hunk of that was to home in on individual goals within his larger Desired Outcome. "A very small piece of the home loan process is verifying home insurance. I spent a week asking myself and every potential source I could find: how do we communicate with six thousand agents around the nation, all of whom are going to do things differently? That became another Desired Outcome, and it took about a week to figure out just that small part of the process. But we did— and then moved on to the next piece of the puzzle. It takes money and time, trial and error. I didn't know that we'd get as big as we are, but I knew that as soon as we figured out the process and discovered how to handle all of that with a system, we'd blow it out of the water."

This experience taught Dan a lot about the importance of developing the clearest possible picture of where you want to go and why you want to get there. He still uses that kind of clarity today to identify Desired Outcomes and drive success in every new marketplace he enters.

Gilbert's a big-game hunter, and not everyone will have the need—or desire—to target DOs as big and beefy as those of the Quicken Loans empire. But *all* of us can benefit from leveraging the process Gilbert used to evaluate his situation, ID his true goals, and form a plan for taking them down. That's consciousness at work—the kind of broad, neutral assessment that can help show the way through even the most tangled issues and challenges.

Scouting: Intel from the Trail

Many of the practices that my hunting lessons have taught me have become almost like natural reflexes. I remember the day this became clear to me. It was late April, and I was walking a ridge that divides a swamp in Antrim County, Michigan. The weather was gorgeous—60-plus degrees and a sky as clear and blue as Lake Michigan. I was moving along at a fast pace, but feeling almost like I was out of my body, totally tuned into everything in my surroundings—watching the sky, listening to the wind, gathering and sorting information about every tree, shrub, animal, and physical landmark I was passing. In other words, I was *scouting*—gathering information and feeding it directly into the data banks of my consciousness. I was drawing heavily on my skill to both detect movement and spot specific shapes and colors to track down some of the best-camouflaged prey a hunter can pursue: black morel mushrooms.

As my trail banked south, I suddenly stopped in my tracks. I'd seen something I needed to pay attention to, but what was it? I scanned the woods around me, and there it was—a massive ash tree hidden behind some pines and cedars, maybe three hundred yards from where I stood. Man, I thought; I must have walked this ridge a hundred times over the years, and I've never noticed that monster. But on *this* hunt I was after black morels, which love to cluster near mature ash trees—and that's why the tree set off my radar. I walked up to the lone giant, and *oh, yeah!* The ground below it was covered in a bumper crop of nearly a hundred black morels. To this day, I've never found a better stash. And I've never lost appreciation for the power—and instinctive nature—of scouting as a True Hunter.

Whether you're on the trail of moose, mushrooms, or more money, scouting is what the hunt is all about. It's the process that feeds your consciousness, by gathering critical information from every conversation, chance meeting, presentation, negotiation, and other event that flows through your world. As a Scout, you won't be someone who sleepwalks through life, failing to see or benefit from all of the opportunity, ideas, and information it offers to those of us who scout with our senses wide open and on high alert.

I've seen over the years how scouting works. It doesn't just uncover the treasures lining your path; it actually brings *more* good things your way. The more scouting you do, the more connections you'll notice among all of the people, ideas, events, and outcomes that flow around you. And tracking down those connections often leads to even bigger, more fulfilling wins than you originally were gunning for. Business deals, friendships, family, personal growth—whatever type of trophy you're seeking, scouting is an essential tool for tracking it down.

So how can you prime yourself to gather the information you'll need to hit your targets and to create a journey that leads to next big win—and the one after that? Here are three basic types of scouting you'll need to master:

1. **Pre-Season Scouting:** The best time to gather information about your hunting territory and the activity of the animals within it is before hunting season begins, when there's less "clutter"—fewer hunters, less competitive combat between animals, and more opportunities to gather real intel about your prey and the territory they're living in. The Pre-Season strategy works when you're scouting out the trail of *any* objective. The more you can learn about broad market trends, emerging competition, and other player developments before you begin negotiating a deal or moving into a highly competitive season or marketplace, the better your chances of walking away with the trophy you're pursuing.

2. **Macro-Scouting:** You need to see the landscape of the territory where you're hunting, and every competitor,

customer, accepted practice, and major challenge roaming there. If you're scouting out new markets for ad sales, for example, your Macro-Scouting will focus on determining who your major competitors for ad space will be, what the buyers are currently looking for, and what trends are catching fire. Macro-Scouting demands stealth and focus. You need to pull in as much data as possible before any other predator *or* your prey knows you're in the territory. If you make a lot of noise before you're ready to act, you're probably going to go home empty-handed—not the outcome you're after. So before you make your move, you need to maximize your visuals, collect all relevant data, and learn about the area you're hunting in—and all of the obvious pitfalls and power positions it contains. Then use the information you gather to get smarter about the challenges and opportunities before you.

3. **Micro-Scouting:** You watch a lot of deer when you're Macro-Scouting. But when you find the one that you want to take, it's time to dig into the details and do your Micro-Scouting. You have to gauge the wind direction so you don't get busted, find the right tree for a clear shot, confirm the actual direction of any tracks to determine the right shooting angle—and find the best way to apply *everything* you've learned from past hunts and observations. If you're Micro-Scouting a business negotiation, be just as detailed: Who has the power to make the final decision in the negotiation? What are they passionate about? What

have their past hunts involved, what are they hunting for now, and what's hunting for *them*? To get this kind of intel, you'll have to get closer to your prey, but go slow and stay small. The hunter who can get in close is going to be the most effective in bagging the trophy. This is why the old saying "You don't see them coming" often applies to the best sales professionals.

Scouting is a weapon that can cut both ways, so you have to learn how to use it well. The more scouting you do, the more data you gather—and the easier it can be to lose sight of what you originally wanted to accomplish with the hunt. You may make a conscious decision to realign or adapt your Desired Outcome based on new information you've uncovered; that's just good hunting.

However, as a True Hunter you *can't* allow yourself to get distracted. Even when you do the heads down, low-to-the-ground work of Micro-Scouting, never forget the big picture—what you came to this hunt to accomplish. If your target is to negotiate a deal, the intel you've gathered should better prepare you to drive the best possible terms from that negotiation. You can't get lazy, stop gathering data, get pulled off track by a target that doesn't really matter, play your hand too early, or drop your guard or your weapons. I've seen more than one broker, salesperson, or account manager work a deal right up to the finish—then blow everything by making a sloppy move at the close (we'll talk more about staying strong right up to the end of The Hunt in Chapter Four). Being a good scout also means having the kind of long-term vision that keeps you on track and headed for real success.

By staying neutral enough to gather the massive amounts of information that life is always throwing our way, we remain open to learning. We see and hear critical pieces of information that we would miss if we were busy ducking for cover. And it's all of that critical data that determines how strong our decisions are and how successfully we act on those decisions—and, in turn, how often we realize our Desired Outcomes. As a True Hunter, you remain aware, maintain consciousness, and continue scouting the best way forward right up to the moment when you take your target. This is a key ingredient for closing the deal in the field or in life.

Seeing Everything: Hunter's Vision

Although successful hunters rarely mention the word "clairvoyant," they will tell you that it's their second nature to put themselves into the mind of their prey—to experience the world through that animal's senses, and to envision the successful outcome of their hunt. And I know that some people aren't comfortable picturing that level of connection to others or being guided by visualization. But I'm also very certain that successful hunters have been using visualization to conquer their prey for tens of thousands of years—painting images of the hunt on the walls of their caves and carving figures of the animals they hunted.

Many hunters have embraced one tradition in particular: they visualize the entire hunt before it takes place, by mentally walking through every step of sighting, tracking, and taking their target.[1] Such a detailed visualization is an essential preparation for *any* hunt—including yours. When you build a clear, detailed picture from multiple perspectives of how your hunt will unfold, the challenges you and other players are likely to meet, the opportunities that you might leverage, and the pitfalls and sidetracks to avoid, then you've drawn up the "able navigator's" map. I call this skill "Hunter's Vision." It's an essential tool that you can develop with practice and that will bring you a powerful weapon for hitting your targets.

Achieving Hunter's Vision enables you to make decisions with your eyes wide open and focused on long-term benefits—the successful outcome you're aiming for. You're not only seeing everything that's taking place in the territory around you; you can also view the world through the eyes of every other creature within that territory. And when you can bring other people's or organizations' perspectives into focus, you can begin to feel what they feel, understand their goals, see their targets. This allows you to predict pretty accurately how they are likely to act—and react—in tight corners and tricky negotiations.

Henry Ford thought so, anyway—he's often quoted as saying that in any negotiation he tried to see the issue from the perspective of the guy sitting across the table.[2] And Henry Ford took the trophy in many of the across-the-table contests he entered into.

All you need in order to use this tool of consciousness is a well-trained mind. Whether you're prepping for a brutal negotiation, developing a critical business alliance, or solving a family conflict, you need to make like Henry Ford and get into the heads of the other people involved in the process. That perspective will feed you some critical information about the hunt ahead, because it will help you to visualize challenges and opportunities from multiple angles. And by wrapping all of that into a visualization of your successful outcome, you are training your mind to:

1. **Anticipate the likely next moves of others and form options for dealing with them.** What are you picking up from the people around you? Is it anger, sarcasm, deceit, or any other ego-driven, fear-based response? When you get a jump on people's fears—or can figure out the prey you're trying to lure in—you're in a better position to pull them into the your target zone.

2. **See the players and the relationships involved, how they fit into the equation, and how they may help or hurt your chances of achieving your Desired**

Outcome. When you've evaluated these elements purely in terms of how they can impact your Desired Outcome, you can use that information to play cautious but deliberate offense.

3. **See the situation with absolute clarity at a macro level, and use that understanding to bring some of the micro pieces into focus.** If you aim small, you miss small. Travis "T-Bone" Turner, a highly successful professional hunter, says that he aims for a particular hair on an animal. Hunter's Vision helps you pinpoint your target with that same level of accuracy. This precision and clarity will help you beat any reasonable quota, deliver on budgets, and hit the bull's-eye of the target you are pursuing.

4. **See your strategic choices and their potential repercussions.** Any action you take is going to move you forward or take you backward—and the latter won't do you any good. This sounds basic, but when I failed to use my Hunter's Vision in the early stages of the WHA, it nearly broke me. Had I forced myself to slow down and think about how others in the hunting industry might react to the tournament I was so happily (and blindly) planning, I could have saved myself a lot of pain down the trail. Lesson learned: Be bold enough to consider *all* possible consequences of your strategic choices.

5. **See the tactical steps it will take to wage your chosen strategy successfully—and begin to choose**

your smartest moves. Hunter's Vision will help you see the path and the trophy it leads to. You'll need to tweak your plan as you go along, but you'll always be moving forward.

Hunter's Vision sets your hunt on fire. Your senses work in harmony and process every new piece of data at a different, more powerful frequency. And hunting at this level puts you in a much better position to pivot as situations demand. Desired Outcomes can and will change, sometimes in a heartbeat. Hunter's Vision keeps a laser focus on the trail ahead, while still allowing you to hold a neutral mind and adapt your Desired Outcomes as situations evolve. You're not wedded to a specific outcome or locked in by your ego. The kind of disciplined flexibility that Hunter's Vision makes possible actually helps you develop better, more solid Desired Outcomes that truly reflect your core desires. As you practice visualizing, remember that every person, place, or event in that hunt holds opportunities that you can exploit, and your visualization needs to help you make sure you don't miss them. These opportunities include:

- **Weakness:** Like Superman with kryptonite, even the smartest buck (or negotiator) has a vulnerability. Seeing the situation from others' perspectives will help you uncover any weaknesses at the table. Consider this information the essential ammunition that you need to have on any hunt.

- **Game-changer moments:** Remember Dan Gilbert's game-changer moment, when he realized he could use technology instead of bricks and mortar to build his Quicken Loans mortgage machine? Much like wild mushrooms in spring, game-changer moment are treasures that can be easy to miss. But when you're using your Hunter's Vision to see the challenge ahead from the perspective of everyone involved, you're much better able to spot pivotal indicators or developments. Game-changers may be signaled by a facial expression, a throwaway comment, or a subtle reaction to a related issue. But even the smallest cue will be easier for you to detect when you are viewing the situation with Hunter's Vision.

- **Controllability:** Most people move through life allowing situations to control *them*, but that's not what drives True Hunters to successful outcomes. When you look at a challenge, deal, or negotiation with consciousness, keep an eye out for signs that others are dropping the reins. Look for any gaps in leadership that would allow you to step in and take control. Remember, our thoughts control our results, so think control, and you will be in control. Most often, it's the internal obstacles that are keeping us from our targets. We can avoid falling victim to such obstacles by staying above the nonsense and keeping a clear, objective mind.

When you're in the woods, Hunter's Vision is just as powerful as all of the trail cams, heat-sensing goggles, scent-masking soaps, decoys, and artificial pheromones that hunters use to find an animal and lure it into the kill zone. The more experienced you are as a True Hunter, the more lightly you can travel. Hunter's Vision is one piece of essential gear that requires no schlepping—and it works in any territory and any season.

I know that I wouldn't be as successful as I am today if I hadn't developed the tool of visualization for tapping into the universe of information and ideas that surrounds us all. This process will prepare you to deal with other people involved in your hunt, because you'll have made the necessary efforts to see the whole experience through their eyes. You're in their heads—armed with some idea of the concerns, objections, and demands they may bring to the process. When you spend time trying to really understand how *they* want the hunt to end, you open your mind to a range of possibilities even bigger than any you've imagined before.

Developing that kind of focus may not come naturally to you; it didn't for me. But Hunter's Vision is one of your most powerful tools for negotiating deals, planning and delivering a pitch, finding and building strong alliances, resolving family disputes, and much, much more. It's a practice well worth the time and energy it will take for you to master it.

A Tool for Visualization

I was a pretty hyperactive kid. By the time I was three years old, my mother knew that I needed some kind of anchor to help focus my attention—ideally, something small and light that I could carry around with me and use at a moment's notice. So she gave me a shoelace, and when I grew too wild, she encouraged me to hold it in my hand and focus on it. And it worked! When I was holding that lace, I could focus my mind on a single idea, which I could develop into a story. As I grew older, the lace became a meditation tool, a tactile object that helped me focus, plan, create elaborate strategies, and imagine their outcomes. I took the lace with me when I went hunting; it calmed my mind and centered my focus by helping me imagine myself in the head of the animal I was tracking.

You need to practice using your Hunter's Vision to visualize and achieve your definition of success. You can find your own visualization tool—a stone, a coin, a key chain. It might even be something you can't hold in your hand, like a specific place or a piece of music; anything that directly taps into one of your five senses of sight, touch, taste, smell, or hearing. Choose a method that will help you focus your Hunter's Vision, and use it in conjunction with the other tools, practices, and techniques we've talked about in this chapter. That practice will help you develop the *sixth* sense of a True Hunter—the ability to get out of your own head, above your ego, and into a state of consciousness.

Fueling The Hunt with Consciousness

Robert Redford is a True Hunter I've always admired, and not just for his award-winning films. Redford has done so much more than acting, producing, and directing in films and on stage. He's also tagged multiple successes as a businessman—as founder of the Sundance Institute, for example, and of the film festival, resort, catalog business, and more that go with it. He's a philanthropist, a mentor, and a make-it-happen advisor for new and independent filmmakers—and he still finds time to be an environmental and political activist.

Redford doesn't get in front of the camera much when he isn't acting, but in interviews or appearances linked to his causes, he comes across as being very still, alert, totally focused on the questions and comments of those around him. Maybe I'm projecting some of his deep-woods character, *Jeremiah Johnson*, into my impression of him—but he seems like a man who's mastered consciousness.

Redford received a career tribute during the 2013 Telluride Film Festival. One reporter wrote in an article that Redford, alert to the dangers of getting locked in the "pretty boy" trap, built his chops as a serious young actor in part by traveling through Europe. There, he had to really watch people carefully and listen to the way they sounded to understand what they were feeling and meaning, since he didn't speak their language.[3] A woman who worked with Redford at Sundance once described his listening style: "He listens in meetings like nothing I've ever seen." She went on to say that Redford starts every meeting with some form of the same message: "My goal in this conversation is to be changed by you. If I walk out with exactly the same perspectives I have now, we have both failed."[4]

What a brilliant way of looking at the world—curious, confident, goal-oriented, and totally attuned to the flow of information and understanding life is constantly sending our way. For me, that openness to life is what consciousness is all about:

- Being present, alive and awake, approaching life as a Scout instead of a Judge
- Staying focused on your ultimate goals as you grow and change
- Gathering the pieces of critical information that life throws in your path—Macro-Scouting the big ideas and Micro-Scouting the small details while holding an observational, neutral mind
- Using a Hunter's Vision to see the hunt from multiple perspectives, to form a clear vision of your Desired Outcome, and to continually guide your actions toward achieving it

You should keep Redford's approach in mind along with your own commitment to consciousness in practice every single day. Remember, if every conversation, meeting, chance encounter, even every observation doesn't change your perspective in some way, you're not paying attention. You're missing important opportunities and therefore failing to grow as a human being—and a True Hunter. If you don't take the time to actually *become* aware—conscious, alive, and alert to your environment—it can be easy to forget about the big picture. Let your ego be your guide, and just struggle through all the undergrowth and dead-end trails that clutter any territory.

Developing and using consciousness is just the first step in becoming a True Hunter. With discipline and practice, consciousness will become your go-to state, the way you live in the world. Think about it, use it, and welcome the changes it brings. That's the kind of outcome we're all aiming for.

The Last Thirty Minutes of Daylight

Whether or not they've completed their hunt, at the end of the day every hunter has to get off the trail and head home. When I find myself in the last thirty minutes of daylight, I know that the time for that day's hunt is running out—and I have to seriously amp up my focus if I want to avoid going home empty-handed.

We've reached the end of the chapter, and I want to be sure you leave this part of The Hunt with something solid. So here are your takeaways from this leg of the journey:

- **Don't be trigger-happy:** True Hunters don't shoot before they hunt. Climb into the tree stand, above your ego and the clutter of circumstance, where you can pull together a big-picture vision of the hunt ahead.

- **Show up in your life:** You see the best path forward toward your Desired Outcomes by *being there*— awake, alive, and alert to the territory around you and everything that's happening within it.

- **Silence the Judge:** Judging doesn't move you forward; it just keeps you stuck in the same old swamp. If you start to feel fear, sadness, or other negative emotions dragging you down, know that it's your ego and not a reflection of reality—so stop *making it* reality. When the Judge starts talking smack, stop listening; instead, focus on the real challenges, opportunities, and events unfolding before you.

- **Get your target in the scope:** Allow your Desired Outcome to drive everything you do. You can't hit your target if you don't have a crystal clear vision of what it is and how to reach it. Know what you want, why you want it, and what success will look like. It should be a measurable achievement, or it's probably not a true Desired Outcome.

- **Better scouting, better hunting:** Scout out the trail toward your outcomes by gathering all of the relevant information you can to fuel your hunt. Get started early, be stealthy and relentless, see and hear and assess your data points. Use Macro-Scouting to bring the big picture into focus, then dive into the small details by Micro-Scouting. Taking the proper prep time to plan out and visualize what is ahead will help you take down your prey more often—every single time.

- **See the win:** Visualization is a powerful tool for True Hunters. When you learn to develop Hunter's Vision, you can see the world through others' eyes and experiences of others. This will allow you to form a detailed vision of how you want your hunt to unfold and to use that visualization to guide your journey through this hunt and on to the next.

KEEPING IT REAL: AUTHENTICITY

Every hunter recognizes the importance of remaining grounded in *reality*. I know I can't get to where I want to go by viewing myself, my business, or the world around me through a filter of fear, greed, or wishful thinking. And I can't rely on the people around me to watch my back if I'm hiding behind so much camouflage that they aren't quite sure where I stand. We make the biggest wins when we drop the camo and engage with reality. When you're hunting from a position of authenticity, your energy and focus are aimed directly at your targets. You have no tracks to cover when you're dealing in facts and acting with clear purpose.

Of course, keeping it real isn't always easy. You have to train yourself to own your strengths and your weaknesses, to be honest with yourself and others about what you want to achieve, and to invest yourself in building and maintaining honest alliances. This is true with relationships, business deals, and the hunt for both personal satisfaction and professional success. You can't make it if you fake it. That's why *authenticity* is one of the pillars of The Hunt method.

Having a unique vision is one thing; sidestepping important truths or blinding yourself to inconvenient facts is a whole other game. You can't form or follow a meaningful vision if you fail to look life square in the face. And there are three areas in The Hunt where having the fewest illusions possible is almost a necessity if you want to land the big targets that bring lasting security and success:

1. **Your nature:** You need to be real—with yourself *and* others—about who you are.
2. **Your targets:** You need to have absolute clarity about what you're hunting for, why you want it, and how you're going to take it.
3. **Your alliances:** You need to be skilled in the care and feeding of the authentic relationships and alliances that can help you in your hunt.

That's it—three elements of an authentic approach to life that will have a major influence on your confidence, your personal impact, and your ability to achieve meaningful success. When authenticity rules these three areas of your hunt, you're on your way to achieving whatever Desired Outcome you've set for yourself—and to being more secure than you'll *ever* be hiding behind layers of camouflage and uncertainty.

I've seen the power of authenticity proved time and again in my life and my hunts. I know how crucial it is to leading effectively, enjoying a powerful network of trust-based relationships, and growing happier and more successful as a human being, family man, friend, and steward of the outdoors. When you face the world with fierce authenticity, you operate from the strongest position any True Hunter can occupy. You have everything you need to get where you want to go. Authenticity keeps you honest about your skills, informed of the risks you face, and prepared to take on the challenges and opportunities ahead. That makes it one of your most powerful tools *and* weapons in The Hunt.

Winning on Your Own Terms

Keeping it real isn't easy. Authenticity can feel like a risky choice in a world where—too often—the numbers are cooked, the information's been spun, and the nugget of gold we're seeking turns out to be nothing more than a shiny object of distraction. We're taught to play life like a game of poker—trust no one, keep our cards close to our chest, and bluff to get ahead. The best hunters are stealthy and masters of camouflage, but they know they can't bluff their way to a win. There's nothing more authentic on this planet than the contest between predator and prey; it's a battle with one winner and a prize of life or death. Animals survive by knowing very clearly what they're capable of doing, and by exploiting their every natural instinct and primal skill. True Hunters have to keep it real at all times, too—no lies, no confusion. That's how you win on your own terms.

Of course, you have to know exactly what those terms mean. You need to know who you are, what you value and believe in, and what you really want out of life. Winning on your own terms also involves having a very clear understanding of what strengths and weaknesses you bring to the hunt. And you can't win on your own terms if you aren't willing to let others see you as you are.

Your authenticity may rattle a few folks, but in most cases, your willingness to drop your guard and own your passions, strengths, and vulnerabilities will make the people around you feel more comfortable. They won't have any doubts about who you are and where they stand with you. In fact, your authenticity gives those around you permission to display their own personal brand—which lays the groundwork for honest alliance, unleashed innovation, and productive collaboration. I rarely have to go hunting for people with passion and solid execution skills to join my organizations or efforts. They come to me, drawn by their desire to be challenged and inspired in a no-game-playing environment where they can help make a real difference in their business and in the world.

A Lion or a Lap Dog?

Authenticity gives you a sense of freedom. When you are up front with the world, you can be who you are and go after what you want, without artificial fears or ego-based insecurities blocking your path. It doesn't matter how much money you have, or how big your house or office is, or how many people report to you; if you can't live an authentic life, you are missing what freedom is all about. You're not a lion, living on its own terms, surviving and thriving through its own instincts and skills; you're a lap dog, quietly sheltering in place and panting for approval. Whatever you're afraid of losing by following the path of authenticity doesn't really belong to you anyway, because

- You have no *real* wealth if you're afraid of losing everything by doing what you *want to do*.
- You have no *real* friends or allies if you're afraid you'll drive away the people you admire by letting them see you as you really are.
- You have no *real* power if you're afraid of losing influence and control by revealing your true goals.

The great thing is that you have a choice. You can be a lion and a True Hunter by choosing the freedom of living your life with authenticity. And when you do, you take your potential off the chain, so you can continue to grow into who you are; to do more of what you want to do; to build stronger, more meaningful relationships; and to get more out of everything that occupies your time.

Stepping Out of the Shadows

We all have our own way of establishing our brand of authenticity. Microsoft founder Bill Gates has become one of the world's leading philanthropists and a social change maker on a global scale. Like his products, Gates's personal brand seems to be all about the business of *getting things done*. But as a quiet, nerdy, even socially awkward individual, Gates never played the role of rising star or trend-setter during all the years he led the charge at Microsoft.[1] People didn't turn to Microsoft for its bleeding-edge style; they came for the sturdy office workhorse products on which Gates built his company's reputation.

Then there was Steve Jobs, whose personal brand was all about design. Jobs was known as a driven perfectionist—maybe even a control freak—who was determined to make sure his company's products would not just reflect modern style, but *establish* it.[2] Jobs infused Apple design with sleek, modern, minimalist profiles and elegant features that appeal to everyday consumers as well as artists, designers, and tastemakers around the world. Apple's products are performance cars, not workhorses, because Steve Jobs refused to accept anything less than the perfection of design and functionality that he'd set out to achieve. Like Gates, Jobs was who he was and built his success on his own terms. Two ground-breaking leaders in technology, two massively successful hunters—with two very different means of expressing their authenticity.

Your style doesn't shape your authenticity; it just delivers it. However, your *willingness* to let others see you as you are drives your arrows toward their mark. You don't have to share every opinion with the folks you work with or lead, or describe every corner of your internal life to the world. You simply live your principles, walk your talk, refuse to compromise your values, and ask for a hand when you need it. When you accept who you are and are willing to let others see *that* hunter, you've started down the path to powerful outcomes.

If letting people see your authentic nature feels risky, here are just a few simple ways you can begin shedding your camouflage:

1. Let's say you finish a meeting or conversation feeling dissatisfied with the outcome. Get above your ego and review your level of authenticity. Did you ask the questions that *really mattered* to you? Were you honest in your opinions and feedback? Did you clearly express the outcomes you were shooting for?

2. Periodically ask others to describe *your* position on an issue; then identify areas where your message seems to be unclear.

3. If you're struggling to resolve a conflict or find an answer to a difficult issue, describe the situation to a trusted friend—or even someone you normally feel threatened by—and ask for their advice.

4. Instead of arguing, ask someone who disagrees with you on an issue or initiative to explain their reasoning, and then *listen*. Remember, authenticity is a two-way street.

Hunting with the Bone Collector

Rather than exposing your vulnerability, standing naked actually can make you bulletproof. When everyone knows who you are, you're free to work your nature for all it's worth. Consider, for example, professional hunter, television personality, and entrepreneur Michael Waddell. Michael is exactly who he appears to be on the program *Michael Waddell's Bone Collector*—a plain-spoken outdoorsman and hunter from Booger Bottom, Georgia, whose love for the hunt landed him a spot on Bill Jordan's *Realtree Outdoors* monster buck hunts and, eventually, his own show on the Outdoor Channel. Michael broke the mold of formal, dry hunting programs. He looked directly into the camera, howled, and threw high fives. And the fans went "Waddell wild." *Bone Collector* quickly became an iconic brand, launching a line of hunting gear and outdoor products that have since brought Michael a whole new breed of "big bucks." And every trophy Michael's taken in his hunt for success has come as a result of keeping it real.

"Nothing has happened by accident in my life," he told me. "I'm proud of who I am. Whether I'm hanging out with

NASCAR drivers, pro baseball players, corporate CEOs, politicians, or just redneckin' it with some of my friends and family, it's all the same to me. You can live like a squirrel, running, hiding, constantly looking over your shoulder to see if an owl or an eagle's coming after you—being the hunted, not the hunter. But I can't live that way, man. Life is all about being real. When you got it, you know it, others know it, and they can't help but be attracted to it."

Michael Waddell walks his talk. Whether you're watching him go after dangerous game or play music with his kid around the campfire, you're seeing the same guy—and his authenticity in action.

Claiming Your Territory

As a Midwestern kid, I grew up by stand hunting. I've spent many hours scouting property, strategically locating a tree stand, and then waiting on a specific buck to cross my sights. I've learned other types of hunting over the years, including still hunting—a method that's common in Western states and involves the groundwork of stalking animals on their trail. But my true "home turf" is made up of the knowledge, insights, experience, and strategic and tactical skill sets I grew up with and developed over my lifetime as a stand hunter. That's my native territory.

Your "native territory" as a True Hunter isn't determined solely by geography or the local wildlife; it's shaped by your personal brand of authenticity. The principles, values, core beliefs about people, business, and relationships, as well as the skills and practices you hone throughout your lifetime give you the confidence you need to calculate the risks ahead and determine the best way forward—or out—in any hunt. That confidence can make all the difference. Great hunters are strategic and tactical, but they listen to their gut as they calculate potential risks and rewards. And your gut reactions will always be strongest when you're keeping it real. Hunting with unflinching authenticity means that you're operating within your native territory and playing to your strengths no matter *where* you are.

True Hunters must get comfortable with the uncomfortable, because they know that's where opportunity often hides. But they also know that some things aren't negotiable. In fact, your beliefs, values, and strengths are the foundation that keeps you rock solid and steady in even a rapidly shifting environment. You claim your territory and grow within it as a hunter by being agile, thinking like a predator, testing and growing your strengths and skill sets, and keeping your focus tightly targeted on your goals. The trail toward your target may have a lot of bends along the way, but as long as it doesn't lead you astray into ideas or actions that conflict with the principles and values that define who you are, you can just keep tracking.

We all change over time. Our ideas expand, our capabilities evolve, our priorities shift, but the core elements of our authentic nature never die. If you've never really thought about your authentic core or your personal brand, now's the time to start. Here's a straightforward way to begin that process: think back to your biggest wins, your best moments, and ask yourself these questions:

1. How did you win? What got you there?
2. What felt like the best, most important part of the hunt?
3. What target did you set out to take, and what motivated you to keep going?
4. What common threads ran through those events that fueled your hunt?

Now, ask yourself the same questions about the hunts that went south. Give this exercise some time, write down your thoughts and answers, then read and repeat as necessary. As you look back at your life, I'm pretty sure you'll discover that the times when you've landed your biggest successes have been when you were playing to your strengths. You were likely tracking down outcomes that mesh with your core principles and values, and being guided on the trail by your authentic nature. I'll also bet that those times when you've gotten yourself in the most trouble were when you weren't being real—when you stretched the truth about your capabilities, ignored your principles, or failed to come clean about something important to your hunt. That's a recipe for disaster. Just like any good brand, we're most successful when we establish who we are and what we stand for. Only then can we claim our territory and own it.

Richard Branson and the Final Frontier

The concept of "native territory" can seem counterintuitive in a world of constant change. But the two ideas aren't really in conflict. Authenticity is about being fearless and confident enough in your personal brand to go after new opportunities, learn to leverage new weapons, and follow new trails as far as you choose to go.

In interviews, in his books, and on his blog, Richard Branson—Virgin Group founder, serial entrepreneur, and global business pioneer—frequently describes his willingness to wade into new frontiers. In fact, he says that taking on challenges in new fields or industries where he's never worked before has played a key role in his successes.[3] He comes in with no preconceived ideas of how things *should* be or how the business *must* be structured. Over the years, he's honed his ability to calculate the risks and rewards that may be waiting in any new territory. Then he can leverage his core strengths and skills to succeed in those ventures, relying on his ability—and that of the people he brings on board—to think like the customers, understand their expectations, and deliver the experiences that will bring them back, time and time again. That's Branson's home turf.

Branson doesn't hesitate to ask other people for their advice and guidance. He hires talented people who seem as down-to-earth as he is, and who can get the "think like the customer" principle that has fueled his success. Then he gets out of their way so they can succeed—and in the process, bring more success to the Virgin brand.[4] Branson even encourages others to say "yes" when new opportunities come their way, and then learn the specifics of making that "yes" a reality as they go. That kind of confident leap is possible only when you've built a deep foundation of skill sets and understand their potential and limitations thoroughly. Banking, airlines, music, nightclubs, even space travel—the Virgin Group has over four hundred businesses under its umbrella, and it's scored major successes in multiple fields. But Branson set the pattern for those hunts early on in his career by getting comfortable with calculated risk.[5] The elements of those calculations are pretty straightforward: Know yourself, know what you're capable of doing, and then leverage everything you've got to go after goals with the fearless determination born of that knowledge.[6]

Marking Your Target

Everyone chokes now and then, and we all long to hide behind camouflage on occasion. But I've found that the times when you most feel like covering up are often the best times to come clean. That means not just owning up to the reality of who you are, but also being bold enough to lay claim to *exactly* what you're shooting for. Remember the photos of Babe Ruth from the 1932 World Series, in which he pointed to the place in the stands to which he was going to drive a home run—a hit that, just moments later, landed precisely where he'd called it?[7] That was a big risk; he could have missed the pitch and been ridiculed for it the rest of his career. But that was Ruth, being who he was—rooted, confident, bold in his actions, and ready to take the fallout, good or bad. That's what marking your target is all about.

I once had a critical A.M. meeting at General Motors World Headquarters, and I was running late. Being late for this meeting was totally unacceptable, and as I blasted south on I-75, I pounded the steering wheel as I tried to think about how to handle it. I'd been up late the night before working on my proposal and—unbelievably—I'd overslept, then couldn't find my keys and had to track them down. In other words, I had no excuse. As I pulled into the parking structure at GM, I briefly considered playing the kid card and saying that I'd had a family emergency, but no—that's not me. And it wasn't authentic.

As I sprinted through the endless hallways of GM's world headquarters, I knew there was only one thing to say. I walked into the conference room, put my iPad on the table, and said, "So I overslept, then lost my keys, and I totally choked, and I feel like a freaking idiot." Five of the seven people in the room burst out laughing, then told me to go ahead and get started. The other two eventually got over themselves, bagged their disapproving looks, and began to focus on my presentation.

I didn't let the fact that I'd potentially weakened my position by showing up late stand in my way. I immediately began explaining my DOs for the meeting: (1) determine whether a two-year media partnership was workable, (2) clarify GM's pricing and product requirements for the project, and (3) agree on payment terms. I wasn't drawing lines in the sand or pushing for one-sided benefits; I was helping to make the meeting more efficient and effective. By first owning up to my lateness and then cutting right to the core of the issue we were there to discuss, I moved everyone past my late arrival and onto the trail of real solutions.

Because I kept my focus, I was able to close the deal—and achieve a game-changing moment for my company. To this day, my partners in that project still laugh about the way I nearly blew the most important meeting in our company's history. I can laugh about it now too, because it really helped me recognize the importance of focusing on the Desired Outcome and forgetting about the noise. Your DOs can be the light that guides you forward when the path is hard to see. But that light shines only when you *own your outcomes* by laying them out clearly and then going after them with everything you've got. That's hunting with authenticity.

Shooting through a smokescreen is no way to get what you're aiming for. You can avoid unnecessary misses by taking a list of one or more DOs into every meeting you lead and then putting them on the table right from the beginning. Not only are you positioning everyone to move toward your goals, but you're also saving everyone's time and showing them the respect of clarity and honesty. Think about how many meetings, projects, or initiatives you've been involved in that turned into a total waste of time just because the person in charge didn't make it clear—maybe didn't even know—what he or she wanted to get out of the effort.

Whether you're creating a mission statement for your organization, outlining quarterly goals for your business, or setting up some kind of workable family budget, you're marking the target you're aiming for by defining your Desired Outcomes. And although it's incredibly important, marking your target isn't complicated. It involves just three steps:

1. **Identify your Desired Outcomes.** Go heads down when preparing for meetings or serious conversations. Take time to form a crystal clear vision of one to three Desired Outcomes that you want to get from any meeting, conversation, collaboration, or other event or action. Your DOs should move you closer to your ultimate, overall personal or professional goals and, ideally,

advance some interest of everyone involved. In my GM meeting, for example, I knew that we had to lock down the essentials of our agreement—details like the time frame, my group's deliverables, and what we'd get from GM in return. Name and list your DOs.

2. **Describe your DOs clearly and concisely.** Now, you have to describe the DOs in the most simple, clear, and complete language possible. Your descriptions need to be dead on, without assumptions, sidestepping, half-finished ideas, or haziness. Remember the exercises you learned in Chapter One for identifying your DOs; ask yourself, "If I get *exactly* what I've described, will it be *exactly* what I want to achieve?" For example, I didn't tell the folks at GM that we needed to "lock down our arrangement"; I specifically described *three concrete agreements* that we needed to make as a result of the meeting. If you're coaching a team member to help boost his performance, you won't be much help if you say, "I want you to improve." Give him something he can sink his teeth into: "I want you to contribute at least one idea in every meeting," "I want you to lead three meetings a month," or "I want to get your follow-up reports within a week of a project's closing." Remember, you're going to be using these descriptions to get other people focused directly on your targets, so you need to be sure that you're accurate and complete—and fearlessly honest. That clarity will ensure that everyone involved knows exactly where they're going

and what they're buying into, which will minimize or even eliminate confusion and conflict down the road.

3. **Search for and destroy any ego-driven elements.** You're looking for results, so before you take your DOs into the hunt, ask yourself: What *kind* of result will each of your DOs produce? If a result is about accomplishing a task, advancing toward a larger target, gaining something of value, or otherwise putting bucks on your pole, then you've got a solid DO. If, on the other hand, your result is all about proving that you're right, putting somebody else in their place, or otherwise feeding your ego, then it isn't worth going after. If you're serious about taking meaningful trophies, forget about fame or justice and focus on *progress*.

Laying out your DOs can be as simple as describing them or handing out a list of them to the people you're dealing with—or as involved as planning a series of meetings to walk everyone through a detailed presentation of clear and comprehensive targets. In tough negotiations, the other side may shake their head and say you're asking for too much. Or they may tell you straight up that they aren't giving in, and you aren't going to get what you want. That's okay; you can negotiate from there. At least everyone on both sides knows exactly where you stand. And if you don't ask for what you want, you're never going to get it.

Of course, every hunt demands a strategy; you have to think about *how* you present your ideas. I didn't tell the DC lobbyists who were gunning for me after the WHA launch, "You're ruining my life. I want you to stop with the personal attacks and negative press, so I can save my business." Instead, I told them that I knew I'd messed up; that I should have consulted with experts in the industry before I launched a major industry event. I made it clear that I wanted to apologize in person and have them see me as who I am, explain my original goals for the WHA, and show them all of the passion and commitment I had invested in the launch. I also asked them how I could channel that energy toward a result we *all* could benefit from. I was asking for their help, while letting them know that we shared some common goals.

You can use the same kind of strategic approach when presenting your own DOs with authenticity. Clearly, you won't get far by saying to a valued but hair-triggered employee, "Man, are you *rude!* You need to stop all the yelling and sarcasm so that the other people on the team are willing to listen to you. You wouldn't believe how much time I spend listening to complaints about you." You have to be absolutely clear and honest in telling such people what you want from them, but in a way that shows you care about *their* success, not just your own: "I want you to become a key leader on my team, so I want to help you get better at communicating your ideas. When you let your emotions go wild, you dilute the value of your message. The important data gets lost, and that doesn't serve you well."

Have you ever been on either side of a tough conversation like that in your personal or professional life? If so, I'm sure you've seen that it's easier to respond positively to caring rather than to criticism. The more important the information you're conveying, the more necessary it is to deliver your message with consciousness as well as authenticity. Consider the potential benefits for you *and* the person you're communicating with; then present your advice in a way that highlights the improved outcomes you want everyone to achieve. We'll talk more about these kinds of fierce conversations later in this chapter.

You'll have a hard time recruiting people to help you achieve an outcome that benefits only you. The most achievable Desired Outcomes have enough flexibility in them to allow for some level of evolution and adaptation, and to produce some form of advantage for everyone. The good news is that the more honest you are with yourself in the process of clearly identifying your DOs, the easier it becomes to be straight with everyone else. That's how you mark your targets with unflinching authenticity. When you do, you build incredibly strong muscles for persuasion and negotiation.

The Truth About Lies

It can be tough to be honest, yet it's central to a True Hunter's nature. Here are three simple truths that will help you keep it real, even when lying seems like the only good option:

- **It's a trap:** You lie only out of fear or ego. Once you begin presenting yourself, your ideas, your DOs in an inauthentic way, you have put yourself in the jaws of fear.
- **It weakens relationships and leverage points:** You might think that you're strengthening your position with allies by pretending to support their ideas or agreeing to pursue an outcome that you won't really put any effort into achieving. However, you're chipping away at the whole foundation that supports your credibility and relationships—which, in turn, form the bedrock for strong leverage points. Weaken the foundation, and everything comes tumbling down.
- **It wastes time and energy:** Though it can be interesting to observe the courting phase of breeding season among animals in the wild, I don't know anyone who enjoys sitting through some elaborate dance around the issues in a board room or serious conversation. Camouflaging your real goals and concerns wastes everyone's investment in your misstated mission—and it can quickly erode the support of everyone you're trying to influence.

Dodging issues, skirting the truth, or even just lying about what you're really after are defensive habits based in fear that we learn when we're kids. And remember: Fear is an ugly trap. The truth, on the other hand, will set you free.

Owning Your Outcomes

Every great hunter is a risk taker. But the best hunters take only well-calculated and timely risks—and they are always prepared to deal with the hard backfire that can result from hunting with a big gun. Hunting with authenticity demands that you pursue your target, even when the hunt grows difficult. You may have to recalibrate your approach to take advantage of shifting conditions and keep a sharp lookout for problems—so you can deal with them before they pile up and block your path forward. And occasionally you'll have to find your way out of a nasty mess that you created or failed to avoid. That's what it takes to *own* your outcomes, which is just as important to your success as identifying them.

Desired Outcomes need to be worthy of the work required to attain them. That means they have to be tied into the heart of what you're actually hunting for. The problems you experience in pursuing a DO often come from a lack of clarity or accuracy in the way you are defining it. For example, I was meeting with a group that specializes in publishing listing information for the government and other entities. This group has a very nice niche business that controls the Michigan market. They came under scrutiny from their board, though, because the type of business that they do is cyclical. It was hot in 2008, '09, and '10, then started to go cold in '11, and continued dropping off through '12 and into '13. To stop the profit hemorrhage, the board of directors gave the group one goal: "We want you to reinvent the business." However, even after months of strategizing they hadn't been able to create a clear path toward that target. Everyone was frustrated; instead of their moving forward, they found that their collective energy was being drained in rationalizing their situation and deflecting blame.

As a consultant, I began by meeting with everyone involved in the reinvention effort, so I could understand the issue from the perspective of the board, as well as from the team that was actually in charge of running the business. They all wanted to know why they were having such a hard time organizing their ideas and coming up with a tactical plan for hitting their outcome. I quickly realized that they were aiming at the wrong DO. The company didn't want—or even *need*—to completely reinvent its business. They'd carved out a niche, an area of expertise in which no one could challenge them; now they needed to create a sustainable model for that niche business, one that would keep them healthy and moving forward in a changing economic environment.

I advised them to examine their existing model to look for potential tweaks that could position their operation to meet some of those cyclical demands and to scale the model into new states during this down cycle where new competitors should not be popping up. Now they had a DO that they could own—one that was squarely within their territory, that they clearly understood, and that they had the weapons to go after. Best of all, the team was able to put together a compelling strategic plan that gained their board's buy-in. Setting the right DO can make all the difference.

When you're working your way through a Desired Outcome, you have to be sure that you've been exceptionally clear about your goals, but you also have to be prepared to deal with whatever comes your way in the process of achieving those outcomes. Denial, blame, backpedaling won't move you forward. When you encounter problems, get back up in the tree stand and view the situation—your DOs and the process you've been following to hit them—without emotion, ego, or any preconceived notions of where you are or should be in your progress. Ask yourself:

1. *Where* did this problem develop?
2. *How* did it develop?
3. *What* does it mean—in other words, how does this problem connect to other issues I'm facing and to the DO I'm pursuing?

Answering those questions will give you the ammunition you need to deal with the problem you've identified. To do that, you need to be concise, fearless, and focused on finding the solution. You also have to be ready to take action on the solutions you've found. Whether it means finding a new process, bringing in new guns, or moving away from people or ideas that just aren't working out, it's your responsibility to make the calls that will keep moving you toward your goal.

In every drama, we play one of three roles: the hero, the villain, or the victim. I always want to be the hero, although sometimes I have to be the villain. But as a True Hunter, I absolutely refuse to play the victim game—and so should you.

Any hunter knows that it's a lot easier to walk into a swamp than it is to climb out of one. But no matter how hard you have to work to claw your way back to solid ground after a misstep, stay out of victim mode. It's a challenge to take on the role of hero in a hunt gone bad, but it's possible, if you maintain your authenticity. Stay cool and lead. Own your mistakes. Talk through the issues, get through the muck, let everyone have a say. Then shut up about what went wrong; draft some new, targeted DOs; and get everyone moving on them. By focusing on real issues, real opportunities, and real solutions, you can help lead everyone out of the swamp.

Building a Pack

A lone wolf can easily take down a rabbit, a sheep, or even a white-tail. But when wolves are going after big prey—a moose or buffalo—they hunt in packs. True Hunters know the value of hunting in packs, too, and they know that the bigger the game you're after, the more you have to rely on your team—whether it's made up of family members, employees, colleagues, or multinational corporations. Great teams aren't just a collection of warm bodies and random skill sets; they're an organized whole, a group of individuals who join forces to go after Desired Outcomes with multiple tools and a single focus. And trust is the glue that holds any team together—trust based on being absolutely clear about every pack member's abilities, interests, and targets.

Building a pack like that takes a real investment of time and attention, and, like any worthwhile investment, it involves a bit of risk. As a hunter, I deal in reality; I am who I am, take it or leave it. When it comes to forging strong alliances, my hunter's authenticity is a calculated risk that has always paid off. By revealing my true nature to the world around me and acknowledging my Desired Outcomes, I've attracted the kinds of people who believe in and support my goals, and I've been able to use those alliances to move more efficiently toward my targets.

I've included the stories of some of those connections throughout this book—people like the visionary business leader Dan Gilbert, VC wizard and change agent Josh Linkner, the boys in the Bone Collector Brotherhood, Realtree founder Bill Jordan, and more. I built every one of those connections on authenticity, with people I know and trust and who know and trust me. We're all happy to lend a hand or watch each other's back in the hunt for success.

On the other hand, we've all known players who put on a big smile and pretend to be in alliances with people that they really don't know or trust. That kind of posing does no one any favors; it wastes time and robs the relationship of any sense of authenticity. Trying to leverage fake relationships is like hunting with bent arrows. You won't get where you want to go if the people you're working with don't trust you.

To assemble a pack worth hunting with, you have to

- Find people who you can communicate with honestly, and who are willing to show the same authenticity in their dealings with you
- Commit to giving as much as you get from the alliance
- Take responsibility for your actions and be willing to call it quits if the relationship moves past the point of repair

Authentic relationships are like weight-training for improved performance. They help you build strengths, knock back weaknesses, and take down bigger targets than you ever could on your own. They give honest clear feedback that comes from a place of admiration and shared goals. But *maintaining* a winning pack is every bit as important as assembling one. Relationships defined by authenticity demand actions as well as words, and a willingness to stand by your commitments. And *nothing* tears a bigger hole in a relationship than failing to take responsibility for your mistakes. The accountability that comes with hunting in a pack is just another aspect of facing the world with authenticity.

Shooting Straight—But Steady

People want to spend time with, work for, and even take criticism from authentic people. Relationships built on authenticity give you much more freedom than you could ever have while trapped in the frustrating game of trying to be someone you're not. Occasionally that means exposing your vulnerability to the pack and asking for help. That kind of bold move shows you're comfortable with who you are and confident in your allies' commitment and capability.

Other times, as we've seen, authenticity demands that you deliver hard truths with sensitivity and compassion. In any case, when alliances are grounded on a platform of authenticity, the people involved are ready to pool their strengths to help track down shared targets. They can use their strongest weapons, knowing that if they misfire or lose sight of the target, another member of the team will give them a hand getting back on course.

Your goal when building a team is to find people who can deal with your authentic nature and who are authentic, too. But that doesn't mean they have to be just like you; in fact, far from it. You want people who are comfortable in their own skin, and who know and can do things that your organization needs, especially the things you're not great at. I'm comfortable taking the lead, handling pressure, making decisions, and moving my teams forward. But I'm not good at finessing the fine details of some initiatives. So I always bring people into my teams who are great project managers and who specialize in organizing essential tasks and monitoring progress. I also staff my teams with creative and reliable foot-soldiers who love to provide the background support and critical grunt work that make any win possible. And in every capacity, I try to surround myself with strong thought leaders— people whose questions and creative drive continually push me and the organization forward. When all of the team members are confident in their skills and comfortable with their roles, none of us has to worry about where we're going or who we're traveling with. And when we have to work out a compromise, forge a new path forward, or find a way to bolt our different ideas together and get them moving as one unit, we understand exactly what kind of ideas we're hooking up with.

Establishing authentic relationships in your personal or professional life might take a few run-throughs. Honesty can take some getting used to, and people who aren't used to dealing with a True Hunter may be suspicious when they first meet up with your naked authenticity. Don't let that shake you. You're standing in your native territory, making genuine connections, and laying out DOs that aren't tied to some hidden agenda. With time, the people around you learn that you aren't just pretending to be real; you *are* real, and willing to let them be real with you, too.

The hard and sometimes uncomfortable work of building authentic relationships is always a good investment. Those are the alliances that put more bucks on the pole—and in your bank account—and get you home, time and time again.

How do you know that you're putting the right dog in the hunt? There are a lot of pretenders in the world, so identifying key strategic partners can be tough. But sometimes what blinds us to reality isn't the other person's camo; it's our own ego. Here are some questions to ask yourself about those you are considering teaming up with:

- Do you need them for a particular strategic or financial reason?
- If they don't partner with you, can you still be successful?
- What is their value today, and what will it look like tomorrow?
- Will they challenge you and make you better?
- Do they bring a unique ability that you lack and that could be critical to your success?

Strong, authentic alliances are not just a weapon, a performance enhancer, a stabilizer. They're also a shield that will deflect a lot of the shots that people outside those alliances will fire at you. People with whom you *don't* have authentic relationships—both real competitors and wannabe's—will take shots at you all time. But when your alliance is grounded in reality, you don't have to worry about anyone you work with—or hunt with or hang with—joining forces with someone who's looking for cracks in your character or operations where they can begin chipping away at your reputation. That's because none of your allies have to wonder who you *really* are and whether you're going to toss them over the wall. As a True Hunter, the relationships that go with that life are a fortress against just about any shots the world might aim your way.

How the Bone Collector Brotherhood Was Born

Shortly after graduating from high school in the small town of Spearfish, South Dakota, Nick Mundt was looking for a way to make a living as an outdoorsman. So when one of his good friends opened a fishing operation in Alaska, Nick left a job in his hometown barbershop and headed north. At the end of the fishing season, Nick came back to South Dakota and took a job as a guide with a hunter's outfitting business. When he began watching hunting shows like *Buckmasters* and *Realtree Outdoors*, he knew he was looking at his future. "That's when I knew I was never going to work in an office, sit behind a desk, or stand behind a barber chair again," he said. "I wanted to be on outdoor television."

So Nick started taking his video camera along on the hunts he was guiding. Not only was he learning to get great footage of the hunt, but he also was building a rep as a savvy, funny expert on the trail—a go-to guide for corporate executives, celebrities, and other professional hunters. It didn't take long before Michael Waddell joined Nick on a turkey hunt in Wyoming; when they clicked, the first part of the brotherhood was born. Michael had Nick on his *Realtree* program a few times, as a cameraman who also spent some time in front of the lens. "I was the sidekick in the camp, and I got to make people laugh," Nick told me. "It took off, and I started developing a following." Rather than being threatened by Nick's fan love, Waddell leveraged it, spending more time with Nick on camera.

Waddell's popularity exploded. "Michael came to me one day and said, 'I'm starting my own brand, and I want you to come with me and help host a TV show.'" Nick's dream had come true, and he had plenty to bring to the alliance—a brotherhood that soon came to include a third member, Travis "T-Bone" Turner.

"The time I spent coming up through the ranks, leading hunts, filming, and getting to meet all of these executives in the hunting industry really helped me," Nick said. "I had a lot of long-lasting relationships. So when we wanted to extend the program and get sponsorships, people welcomed us with open arms." Within just a few years, *Michael Waddell's Bone Collector* was the biggest show on the Outdoor Channel lineup.

The authentic pack that the three Bone Collectors had formed became the foundation for a success that was bigger than any of them had imagined. "It all just boiled down to building relationships," Nick said. "Not only as a hunter, but as somebody who could connect with people in an authentic real kind of way. That's what the brotherhood is built on."

Staying True

Nature is a great equalizer. As my hunting partner Jeff Paro likes to say, "Whoever you dress up as in business each day means nothing in the wild." Paro's right; as far as a grizzly bear is concerned, you aren't a rock star, CEO, or senator; you're just a tasty meal with two legs. A huge corner office or hefty bank account back home won't keep you alive.

That's why so many hunters have such authentic relationships. The bone-deep connections you form in nature often stay with you throughout your life. When you're hunting together, your relationship moves to a whole new level, your conversations take on new meaning, and you start thinking about deeper possibilities for your partnership. True Hunters know that in order to keep that bond tight, they have to stay as true to their alliances as they are to their core principles and beliefs.

Long-term relationships are living things that demand care. Of course, you don't have to throw constant attention at real relationships. You can speak with an authentic friend or a business ally once a year and still manage to keep your bond as tight as if you were connected on a daily basis. But authentic alliances can't survive without loyalty—the kind of commitment that says, "When you need me, I'll be there. If you want the truth, I'll tell it to you. If I say I'll do something, I'll do it." That's a True Hunter's commitment—one that always serves you well.

Of course, hunting can take us into difficult territory, where events can cloud even the most solid connection. When a shadow falls across one of your critical alliances, remember that the Judge is not your ally; rather, it's the Scout who will help you maintain strong relationships. You have to get the data in before you make decisions or take action. People who willingly throw their friends or allies overboard are afraid of drowning themselves. They're thrashing around, ready to grab anything that floats by, willing to stand on anyone's head in order to keep their own chin above the water. True Hunters know that they can't let that kind of desperation guide their actions. They don't allow fear, anger, guilt, and other negative emotions to lure them away from their authenticity and into indecision and knee-jerk reactions.

The best way to avoid bad endings in your hunt for solid alliances is to deal with issues honestly and unemotionally from the beginning. You'll face some uncomfortable moments, but that's routine maintenance for authentic relationships. Step one, of course, is all about consciousness—getting above your ego and gaining clarity. When you face an issue or situation that threatens a critical alliance, take some time to get up where you can see what's really going on. Be as neutral as possible while observing the people and events around the issue in their own light, not just in terms of how they affect you.

After reflection, it's time for step two—action. You have to demonstrate respect for your partners or team by actually confronting the behaviors or ideas or issues that are undermining the strength of your mission. That's a process that demands authenticity.

In her books and workshops, author and leadership development coach Susan Scott encourages those who want to improve their skills in alliance-building to get comfortable with what she calls "fierce conversations."[8] Scott's message is all about how to have real, meaningful communications with people, even about heavy emotional subjects. I've learned a lot from Scott's work, but perhaps the most important takeaways for me are these guidelines for talking over difficult issues:

1. Always keep tough conversations *factual and authentic.*
2. Always keep your desired outcome for the conversation *clearly defined and targeted.* Avoid gray areas, which can cause blow-ups in tough interactions.

When daylight opens up between you and an ally—a friend, your spouse, a team member or business partner—you're going to have to talk about it. Those conversations deserve just as much attention and prep work as you'd give to important business negotiations. Every tough talk is its own animal, but here are some guidelines that will help you overcome any of them:

1. Before your conversation, determine what you want to happen—how you want things to change.
2. Go into the talk armed with straight facts and authenticity. Leave your ego outside.
3. Lay out your concerns and state your Desired Outcome, then ask the other person for his or her take on the issue.
4. *Listen* to what the person has to say.
5. Stay cool and keep your DO for the conversation clearly defined, so there is no gray area. And *always* keep your words and actions targeted at moving forward.
6. No matter how many of your buttons the problem is pushing, focus on results—not emotions.

Even small disagreements can bog down alliances. The good news is that learning to work your way through nasty spots along the way can make your bond with the folks sharing your journey that much stronger. And if you don't make it to the other side together, you can

know that you didn't just wander away from a relationship that mattered.

Tagging Out an Alliance

Not every hunt will end in a trophy. Sometimes you just
have to tag out—walk away and get ready for the next day's
hunt. And every alliance you form won't be a keeper, either,
no matter how much you want to maintain it. Interests,
goals, and circumstances change, so you may find yourself
with a partnership that no longer works. Ending an alliance
is never fun, or even comfortable, but it's kind of like going
in and getting a vaccination as a kid; brief pain, with lasting
benefits. You just have to suck it up. If people can run Iron
Man competitions, donate a kidney, or climb Mt. Everest,
you can certainly overcome your desire to bolt when it
comes to closing the door on a dysfunctional relationship.

I once was forced to part ways with a critical player in
one of my companies. He had been my technology partner,
someone I respected who had earned huge professional
success. We'd always differed in our core philosophies and
beliefs around business, but I had just skirted around those
differences because I liked this guy and I thought my business needed his expertise. He sidestepped the issues, too,
because he loved his work.

Eventually, however, our avoidance maneuvers had
taken us so far off the path of authenticity that we
had totally lost our way forward. By the time I finally

brought the relationship to an end, we'd played so many mind games with each other that it was almost impossible to go back and have an authentic conversation about anything, let alone the reasons behind the breakup. I realized that I couldn't work with this guy any longer, and I couldn't even be friends with him. There was no way to go back and clean up all the garbage that we'd accumulated in our relationship. We could have avoided that mountain of ugliness if we'd fearlessly confronted our differences from the beginning and honestly discussed how—or even *whether*—we could overcome them enough to form an authentic partnership. The whole mess was an ugly lesson for me.

Now, think back to some of your own ugly breakups—whether they happened at work or in your personal life. Did *any* of them come about as a result of a relationship built on a foundation of honesty and authenticity? How often have you felt an alliance suffocating under the slow accumulation of one overlooked or unspoken issue after another? You might be able to postpone uncomfortable confrontations by keeping important facts off the table, but that's no way to fight off alliance-killing doubts or events. In fact, you're just feeding the beast. If you've examined the data and realize that to make the highest and best use of your resources, you need to remove a direct report from a position of power and replace him or her with someone else, it's time to call on your authenticity.

Sit down with the person and lay out the facts. Explain the *real* reason you're making the change. Sure, it's tempting to claim that your business model has changed or the market has shifted or whatever other "safe" excuse you can come up with. But that's like putting electrician's tape over a dashboard warning light; it is not going to fix the problem. Just wait until the guy you bumped does a little research and finds out the truth you were hiding; then it's going to get really ugly. When you step up to tough endings with understanding and unemotional truth, you can come out of even the most brutal breakup with relatively solid shared respect and positive results. People don't have to wonder what you're *really* thinking, because they know the truth.

How do you begin these difficult conversations? Remember the steps for any tough conversation, then be prepared tell it like it is—with consciousness and authenticity:

1. Before the talk, identify what you want to get out of the conversation and write down your DOs, as usual. Then think about each of them from the perspective of the person with whom you'll be speaking.

2. Now write down what you think the outcomes will achieve for you and your friend, partner, or ally. What's motivating you to hit those targets? If ego plays a role, face it and understand why your ego is shouting on this

issue. Remember, authentic results don't rest on pride or insecurity or a need for revenge. If your motives are driven by ego, you need to check yourself before you wreck the relationship.

3. When you go into the meeting, take the DOs and the reasons behind them in with you and lay them out clearly—without shame, double-speak, or anger. Then let the other person respond. Listen carefully and think about what you're hearing. Does this response in any way shift the points you've already reviewed?

4. When (not if) emotions start to rise, go back to the reasons you've established for initiating the split, but don't engage in a long, protracted argument. You don't want to be cruel and dismissive, but at the same time, you don't want to venture down a trail that might lead to ugly exchanges that you and your one-time ally will both regret.

These are guidelines, of course. No important relationship can be managed, or ended, by the numbers. Sometimes the conversation sparks some new understanding or insight that truly changes the target for you. But if you've considered this conversation with consciousness, done the Scouting necessary to pull in all relevant data points, and assessed your motivations with absolute authenticity, then you've done the groundwork necessary to handle any difficult conversation as cleanly as possible. I promise that as you become more comfortable hunting with authenticity, you'll become better at forming alliances that are good for the long trail ahead—and at bringing a clean ending to those that can't make it through The Hunt.

I knew I was making the best move for the organization in terminating my tech partner. However, I also knew that I had set up a hard fall right from the beginning. I didn't set the right expectations, I hadn't raised the concerns as I saw them developing, and I sidestepped those uncomfortable conversations. I allowed "the gray" to enter. When it comes to communication, authenticity requires transparency, clarity, and the high resolution of black and white.

Now, all of that high-definition communication doesn't make you bullet-proof. You won't always be right in your decisions; people won't always hear what you intend to say. But when you're hunting with authenticity in partnership with the other pillars of The Hunt method, you'll never have to worry that you needlessly struck a fatal blow to a relationship that you might have been able to save with just a little more thought and effort.

Shedding Camouflage

Keeping it real isn't easy. I've run a few early-stage companies that I've been blessed to see find their way to success. Over the years, I've learned that the most dangerous lies are the ones we tell ourselves about all of the reasons that we *can't* hit our targets. And once those lies take hold, they're hard to shed. Those negative messages or hidden alibis just keep firing in our heads, until false modesty or fear becomes our reality.

For a deer hunter, the trap can feel like this: You're in a tree stand, the weather's turning ugly, and you can't get out because you're going to spook any deer that might be around—so you just have to sit there and think. But it's not a healing kind of self-reflection, because you're thinking about the same negative garbage you've been thinking about since you were fifteen years old—all the things you *can't* do or *should* do on this hunt, all of your regrets. Suddenly, you're not a predator. You're a depressed, uncertain human being, clinging to the side of a tree and hoping that some animal is unlucky enough to get in the way of your arrows. When you hit that stage, you might as well crawl down the tree and go home, because you're done hunting for that day. Your focus, skill, and determination are done.

When you feel the grip of fear starting to pull you down, you can slide down into its trap and kiss success goodbye. Or you can get back to The Hunt. The next time you find yourself starting to play that loop of negative messaging, fight the fear by *reminding yourself of who you really are*. Remember the tools at your disposal and the weapons you've used effectively in the past. Believe in your skills as a True Hunter. Go ahead and expect that things are going to go *right* for you. You've already taken the hard step, right? You *already have* the office, the relationship, or the responsibility to perform. That's how to take the first step out of the shadows—to begin shedding any camouflage of negativity and fear that you've grown accustomed to wearing. You were born with the potential to become a True Hunter. That's the reality you want to live in, and the territory you'll rule when you hunt with unflinching authenticity.

The Last Thirty Minutes of Daylight

Here are the key ideas from this chapter that you need to pack with you on The Hunt:

- **Start with a desire to be real.** Be fearless when it comes to owning your true nature.
- **Be clear—with yourself and others.** Leave no gray areas in your communication, philosophy, or objectives.
- **Learn and develop your unique hunting style.** Hone your own brand of unflinching authenticity and then live it.
- **Master your native territory and weapons.** Learn the fundamentals, know the variables, leverage your strengths, and minimize your weaknesses, so you can hunt from your strongest position.

- **Own your desired outcomes.** Lay out your targets so that everyone understands them, right up front. Then take responsibility for hitting them.
- **Stay real by staying in consciousness.** Be conscious, aware, and reflective.
- **Invest in authentic relationships.** Be real with people and give them permission to be real with you, so that even when the hunt heats up, you have an authentic pack watching your back.
- **Get comfortable with uncomfortable situations and conversations.** You can't be authentic if you're unable to deal with and deliver hard truths.
- **Always be on the lookout for ego.** Control it or it will control you.

TAKING TROPHIES:
LEVERAGE

I've learned some valuable lessons as a result of tough times in business, and the power of *leverage* in The Hunt is high up on that list. I've always been conscious of the difference between leaders and followers, but I'd never really appreciated the pull of the herding mentality, especially in more traditional industries such as hunting. When I was able to look back unemotionally at my lone-wolf approach to the WHA—keeping my plans secret from the big dogs in the industry, cooking up elaborate money giveaways and promotional teasers, then springing up out of nowhere with a glitzy media launch—I couldn't help but laugh about how far off-target I had been. But I stopped laughing when I thought about how quickly the campaign against me and the WHA had spread. The outdoor world's online ecosystem was a lot more muscular than I could have guessed, and the industry lobbyists certainly knew how to leverage it.

But when I took the time to scan the endless web pages of the forces aligned against me, I realized that I was looking at a leverage point I could use, too. I knew that I had to own a good portion of online real estate that would allow me to activate a message, power a brand, and move the herd in whatever direction I wanted to take it. That would put me in the alpha position.

Step one, though, was to find some way to bring the WHA back to life. Through a number of phone calls and visits, I'd begun the process of disarming the industry lobbyists who'd been gunning for me. Now, I knew I had to offer up the only real leverage point I held. I let them know that if they worked with me, I'd move the tournament to a traditional format and take the animals in a traditional way. I had no idea how my investors would feel about the move, but my hunter's instincts told me I had to take it. I needed a win, and I had limited weapons. Using this one would get me back in the hunt. And it was the only possible path for getting my business *and* my investors on the path to profit.

Am I an opportunist? No doubt! All animals are; that's how we survive. Life is tough and unpredictable, so animal instincts are targeted on leveraging every opportunity in the environment. The best opportunists get the most food, hook up with the choicest mates, find the safest shelter, and avoid the fiercest predators. In other words, opportunists rule the pack.

Great hunters have to be ultimate opportunists. They know how to use every skill, experience, person, place, idea, issue, or event to move closer to their target. To thrive in any environment, you have to exercise your instinctive ability to scout out and use every opportunity that comes your way. That's why True Hunters master the critical skills of leverage, including

- Exploiting your **unique nature** as an individual
- Exercising the **predatory wisdom** you inherited as a human being
- Developing an **instinctive impulse to build and use a powerful network** of people, organizations, events, and ideas

It took me thirty-nine years and some deep conversations with trusted colleagues and mentors to realize it, but ninety-nine times out of a hundred, there's a winning path wide open before us if we know how to find and leverage opportunities effectively. Leverage creates intersections between people, places, and issues that build strong success and push you toward the *flow* state of intensely focused and hyperproductive performance. Instinctive leverage extends your reach, amps up your power, and enables you to do more than you could even imagine doing without it. Think of it as the fuel that keeps the wheels of business turning.

Let's say you work in real estate. You could raise $20 million and, with the right financial leverage, turn that fund into $80 million or even $100 million worth of deals. Creating and building on the right relationships might allow you to bypass endless phone calls and superfluous meetings and to gain direct access to the power brokers you need to deal with. If you're on the trail of the biggest whitetail of your life, you'll take it only if you are able to spot and exploit every potential piece of cover, sight advantage, and wind change. True Hunters know that leveraging opportunity isn't wrong or greedy; it's authentic. And it's the key to taking trophies on The Hunt.

Leveraging Your Nature

Here's some good news about getting better at The Hunt: You already have the most important tool for upping up your personal performance. In fact, you were born with it. I'm talking about your *unique nature*, which is your go-to arsenal for any hunt. Every human is born with the instincts and skills of a super-predator, but that birthright alone won't make you a successful hunter. Before you can pull everything around you into sharp focus, you have to get clear about your own nature—who you are, what you're capable of doing, and how you can tap both your strengths and weaknesses to advance toward your target. By understanding your capabilities, the things that turn you on or off, and the seasons and cycles of your performance patterns, you position yourself to leverage every weapon you're packing to achieve peak performance, every time. When you know what you uniquely bring to The Hunt, you can use it for all it's worth.

It can be tricky to get a handle on your nature—something I remembered when I sat down to meet with Kyle, a member of my team at OutdoorHub. I'd hired Kyle to help OHub bring all of its video assets and web publishers together, so we could create a multichannel partnership with YouTube, which would be an incredible monetization opportunity for us. We had brought in Kyle to set up the program, digitize the first five or six hundred videos, get them ready for the Web, and then grow out this area of our business. But just five months after starting the job, Kyle had turned in his resignation. In his exit interview, I was determined to find out why.

I'd been watching this guy work, and I thought he was really sharp. I'd lined up a number of plans for leveraging his talent in the months ahead, which I told him as our meeting got under way. I asked him to talk to me about why he was leaving. Kyle quickly tracked back through the past decade of his career—basically, telling me about every job he'd had since college. He wanted me to know that he'd *never* had a job that worked out. He said he had no real explanation, but he'd jumped from one thing to the next so much that he'd never made any real progress in his professional life.

"Really?" I asked. "Haven't you been able to leverage *any* of those experiences?"

The question just seemed to confuse Kyle, so I dug in a bit further with some simple questions about his work at OHub: Did he learn a lot about setting up a multichannel platform on YouTube? "More than I could have ever imagined," he answered. Did he learn a lot about developing an idea into a reality, by scouting out all of its assets and using them to build a platform? "Oh yeah," he said again, "without a doubt." So, could he take those multichannel platform skills to another level, another channel—something that could help him with his career as TV continues to trend toward an online life beyond cable?

Kyle was nodding to show me that he got where I was going. But then he looked down at the floor and kind of reluctantly admitted to me that the biggest reason he was leaving was so he could go freelance—sit at home in his underwear, work when he felt like working, and earn the same salary he was making at OHub in about a third of the time. "The only reason I made it for five months instead of five weeks was because I was questioning all of those past times I'd walked away from a good job," he added.

"Okay," I said, "let's clear some things up. First, I'm not upset with you for leaving. I can leverage the platform you started building here—the logo, the watermarks, the stuff you digitized, the process you put in place. I'll staff it with a young kid fresh out of school who's hungry to get into video and will keep moving the work forward. But I'm curious: why did you take me on that walk through your career history—the story about how you 'just can't stick with a job'?"

I could tell that Kyle was starting to get lost again, so I yanked him back to the central issue: "I totally get why you want to go freelance—hey, I'd be happy to use you on a contract basis. But you gotta stop acting like a victim of your nature. You are who you are, man—stop fighting it and start using it!"

Kyle's expression changed from confusion to clarity. I think he finally felt free to follow the path his personality had been pushing him toward since he'd left college. He didn't have to apologize to me or regret the fact that he couldn't fit into an office environment; he just needed to own it and use it to move his own hunt forward, toward his own targets. And he had about ten years of on-the-job training and experience he could leverage on that hunt, too.

Kyle and I have continued to work together on a contract basis, and he seems like a whole new hunter—happy, confident, more in charge of his life. I hope he always remembers who he is and what he's hunting for.

Now, I don't think Kyle lied to me about his commitment when he took the job at OHub. I think he was lying to *himself*, sleepwalking through his life, putting in time at one office job after another and doing what he guessed he should be doing, instead of getting clear about who he really is and using that clarity to build the life he really wants. Understanding and leveraging your unique nature doesn't require that you leave everything behind and stalk off on some lifelong vision quest through the desert. But it doesn't give you a license to rape and pillage your way through life, either. Hunting with leverage simply demands that you look at yourself and your life with clarity and then use what you see to get where you want to go.

We all know where that hunt begins: up in the tree stand of consciousness. You need to put yourself above the noise of conformity and common wisdom and all of those illusions about what *should be*, because none of that is reality. When you can see the world as it really is, you'll be able to see yourself clearly, too—your life and all of your past experiences (good and bad); the things you're drawn to and the things that you despise; what you're good at, and what you struggle with. Then you can own and use every aspect of your nature you've identified. Everyone has "soft spots"; by coming to grips with yours, you'll be better able to connect with a difficult client, understand an angry teenager, troubleshoot a dysfunctional work process, avoid a bad outcome, or propose a better strategy.

You need to abandon the idea that you can "fix" your nature; you can't. But you *can* know and leverage every aspect of it. Then the personal growth, the getting better, the "fixing" will happen all on its own. You'll be operating at peak performance levels, and there's nothing more you can ask of yourself—or anyone else.

Clarity: The Root of All Leverage

Quicken Loan founder Dan Gilbert always says, "Nothing clarifies like clarity." I repeat that expression a lot, and I've seen how its simple yet incredibly powerful message tends to skate right over the heads of people who aren't really listening. Clarity helps you get a tighter grip on every aspect of your life. And leverage is impossible without clarity. If you don't know what you want, you can't possibly know the best way to get it.

Early in my career, I had the blessing and curse of working with my father, who brought me right from school into his real estate business. Not long after I started working for him, Dad made me a property manager and handed over a tough portfolio of properties. That morning, we sat down in his office and he asked me: "What is your job as the property manager?"

I knew this one! I began to tick off the list: "Making tenants comfortable. Making sure the properties are in the right shape. Making sure leasing signs are up. Making sure everything's right—"

"Stop it!" Dad said. "What is *your job* as the property manager?"

We did this a couple more times—him asking, me stumbling through my answers, until finally I got it. "Wait," I said. "My job is to collect the rent."

"Yes," he said. "Your job is to collect the damned rent, whatever it takes. Everything else you do as a property manager is merely leverage that helps you collect the rent. And the minute you don't understand that, we're screwed. At the end of the day, either you will have done your job or you won't. Banks don't care about all of the other wonderful things you're doing if you aren't collecting the rent."

My dad was helping me get the same kind of clarity Dan Gilbert talks about. When you're clear about what you're hunting for, you absolutely will know how to find and use every leverage point available to help take your target. That's your job, hunter—and nobody should know it better than you.

Tracking Your Season

Every hunter knows there are specific times when animals are more active. For the most part, those periods depend on the position of the sun and the moon in relation to earth. Dusk, dawn, midday—those solar positions have a daily influence on all animal behavior. They determine when animals sleep, hunt, mate, and search for food.

The moon has its own gravitational pull on all of us animals here on earth. The full moon is a bow hunter's kick-back time. We can sit around, talking and drinking beer late into the night, because the deer we're after are active just about all night—out courting, fighting, and generally living large under that big, bright moon. They aren't going to be up and at it early in the morning, so we don't have to hit the woods early, either. On all other days, I know that the three-hour period around dawn is the most likely time to find animals actively moving, looking for food or mating opportunities. So if the sun rises at 7:00 A.M., I'm going to be in my tree stand well before 6 A.M. and on hyper focus until 9:00 or 10:00, without fail.

If you think that the seasonal or cyclical aspect of the natural world doesn't hold much sway in your own life, you're wrong. We may have replaced our knowledge of the sun's position in the sky with an alarm clock, but our instincts are finely tuned to natural cycles, and we respond to those on a gut level, not through our intellect. Some of those cycles come with the package: human fertility cycles coordinate with the lunar phases, and the sun's position plays a role in shaping human sleep patterns. Other cycles are based in our own unique nature, on what our own "internal clock" tells us about our performance curve—when we should be up, when we should hit it hard, and when we should be kicked back and recharging our mojo. Every piece of understanding you gain about your unique natural performance patterns offers a potential advantage for you in The Hunt. When you know how to leverage your natural cycles and peak periods of performance, you improve your chances of taking the trophies you're after.

I have always been an early riser. My passion for hunting and fishing just cemented that early morning aspect of my nature, because it forced me to be up before the crack of dawn, even on days when I didn't have school. And though I learned everything I could about animal peak activity periods, I didn't give much thought to my own.

As I began to grow in my professional life, though, I realized that I was pacing my day around my own unique rhythms. I was up around 4:00 every morning, and by 5:00 I was ready to tackle the tough stuff—the grittiest jobs of my day—during that early morning time slot. Fortunately, those are hours when most of the other humans I work and live with are focused on their own morning rituals, so I'm working at my best *and* without interruption. I can do ten times the work during those hours than I can do at any other time during the day. When I gained that clarity about my performance patterns, it changed everything about the way I approach my job and plan my day.

To get the most benefit from your own *peak activity window*—let's just call it your PAW—you need to identify those hours and then leverage them to tackle your most demanding work. The artificial schedules by which we live can make our daily peak activity windows harder to recognize and use. Although our schedules tend to be controlled by outside forces, our natural cycles are strictly internal—which makes their pull much more powerful. Many people can do their strongest cognitive work in the morning, when they're fresh and have higher energy and clarity. But that may not be *your* hunt. Your PAW may run for two hours, starting at noon, or you may have a five-hour period of daily peak performance that starts at 7:00 P.M. and runs to midnight. You might even have one two-hour period in the morning and another at night. No matter when your specific PAW begins and ends, you definitely have one. And when you can identify and leverage it effectively, you have a ticket to getting a *lot* more accomplished in a *lot* less time.

You don't want to waste your PAW by using it to clear out boring, blah-blah, check-the-box work. You can do that when the phone's ringing, people are running in and out of your office, the kids are yelling for your attention, or the construction crew is just starting to do the rehab next door. Instead, use your PAW time to take on work that demands critical thinking and heads-down concentration and decision making. When you're in that PAW, your ability to think clearly and see the best path forward is at its peak, too.

So how do you identify the most productive hours in your daily pattern? You can start by using your hunter's consciousness. Be the Scout and track yourself through the day. Gauge your moods as well as the quality of the work you're turning out. When you realize that you've just plowed through tough tasks with relatively little pain, note the time. When even the simplest tasks seem difficult, note that time, too. When do you find yourself finally taking on the jobs that you've been putting off for days? And how did that work go for you? Look at the type of thinking you find yourself doing at different times of the day, too. You might find that you want to take on those big, cognitive tasks early in the day, but that you're better at creative work late in the evening, when your brain is starting to unspool from the demands of others and you're better able to focus on abstract ideas. Tap into your authenticity to be very clear about what you're doing, when you're doing it, and why. By scouting out your performance patterns, you can leverage that knowledge by matching the kind of work you have to do with the best times for you to do it.

Don't expect to be able to revolutionize your results in a heartbeat. It will take time to get with the rhythm of your new schedule. And don't push it. You can't stretch your PAW beyond its natural borders so you can go full-bore on mind-bending work all day—that will fry you out. Just find your pattern and then go with it. Remember, you are an animal, not a machine. As much as we *have* to march to other people's schedules sometimes, we will never be at our best when we ignore the patterns of our own nature.

Over time, as you begin matching your schedule to your natural rhythms, you'll find your daily peak performance pattern. I promise that the change will do you good.[1]

Guarding Your Treasure

I was recently in a meeting with the staff and COO of one my companies. I'd listed the Desired Outcomes for the meeting right off the bat, but instead of digging into them, the team started getting hung up on a bunch of personality issues—this client, that vendor, that guy who runs that other company. They were bringing up things that had nothing to do with the reasons we'd come together for the meeting.

I let it go on for about eight minutes, and then I interrupted the dish session. "We have fifty-two minutes left in this meeting," I said, "and a big agenda in front of us that we have to tackle. Seems to me, though, that we sound more like an episode of *Gossip Girl* than a company trying to nail its priorities. I know all this trash talking might seem relevant, but unless it has something to do with the DOs that we've laid out, I suggest we stop talking about other people and start talking about solutions and what we'll need to do to make them happen."

I'm happy to say that no one in the meeting wasted another minute defending their time-killing gossip fest. We just got down to work.

Time and energy are two of your most precious resources for the hunt; you need to value and respect them. And even though these two commodities are very different, they're pretty closely linked. Time is an external force, determined by the solar cycle and outside our control; energy, on the other hand, is ours to build and burn. The way we use one directly affects the other. Our level of energy determines how we make use of our time, and the way we use our time shapes the payback we get from our energy expenditures. To get the most possible leverage from our time-and-energy treasury, we have to remember a piece of advice I handed out early in this book: *Don't confuse activity with results.*

As you begin scouting out your performance patterns, I suspect that you'll be surprised by how much time you flush away every day. I'm not talking about down time. We all need time to just stare out the window and think, or to occasionally take the longer, more scenic route on the way to whatever end result is in front of us. Getting clear, scouting, fueling up for the next leg of the hunt—spending that kind of time can bring hefty returns.

On the other hand, here are just a few of the ways you can waste time:

- Procrastinating
- Endlessly rehashing a situation and stalling on making the call, even when you know what the right decision is
- Stomping around in guilty feelings about the past without actually learning anything new from it

- Digging into the dirt of other people's lives just for the sheer pleasure of it
- Constructing and maintaining a false image
- Being driven by envy, bitterness, greed, or some other negative force

Most of these time-killers are born in ego. You're acting uncertain because you want to feel justified about something you can't really justify. You're circling around *this* because you're stuck on *that*. Wasting time can feel a lot easier than actually moving forward: "Well, I *could* work on getting my taxes together. *Or* I could spend the next hour complaining about why my taxes are so high." You don't need me to walk you through the pros and cons of that kind of decision. Just remember this: You can't hunt like a master if you are a slave to your fears.

Guarding your time requires that you rise above your ego and get clear about just what it is you're hunting for. Then you can target your actions on hitting those DOs, rather than getting caught up in useless time-wasters with no real return. If you're hunting whitetails, for example, you've got one great morning sit—those first few hours when the deer are up and active. If you're still scrambling to get on the road when daylight hits, you might as well stay home. In fact, taking it easy must have been more important to you than hunting. When you're clear and honest about what you *really* want to get out of your time, you'll know where you need to invest your energy. That's one of the most important ways that you leverage your nature.

Preparation is another necessary tool for guarding your time. That means doing the prep work necessary to make a quick, clean kill of the object you're after—the deal, the promotion, the new budget, whatever. Being prepared means that you position yourself to be in the right places at the right time and then leverage every opportunity that presents itself in that moment.

Protecting your PAW is critical for conserving your time and energy, too. When people become aware of your work cycle, you can become a sitting target. You don't have to give distractions a shot; let everyone know when you're unavailable, and then *be unavailable*. It's not always easy to carve out limits like this; but then again, turning in peak performance isn't ever going to be easy. No matter how many people and issues are competing for your attention, it's your job to defend your time.

Of course, we're often our own worst enemy when it comes to time wasting. We can become so used to spending hours of our day caught in time-killing traps that we don't even notice them anymore. So take a good long look at how you're spending your time. Once you've formed a clear picture of any time-wasting habits you've developed, create a list of ways to avoid them and post it where you can see it every day. Here's an example:

- Don't get distracted by email, gossip, or other shiny objects.
- Stay focused on your DOs.
- Learn and leverage your peak activity window.
- Be honest about why you're doing what you're doing.
- Don't meddle in coworker conflicts or other situations where you have little chance of adding sustainable value.
- Know how to say no—to yourself and others. This is freedom.

We're never going to be perfectly functioning time organizers, but perfection isn't the point—discipline is. That's what it takes to use your time and energy wisely and, in fact, to leverage any aspect of your nature. Just as we make a habit of brushing our teeth, all of us can make a habit of controlling what kind of junk we expose our brains to and the kind of time sinks in which we indulge. But there are plenty of really worthwhile investments you can make with your life—family, relationships, personal growth, long-term goals, community. Guarding the most valuable commodities you control—your time and energy—is a habit worth developing.

Leveraging a Hunter's Wisdom

Years ago, early in November, I was at the farm up in Ellsworth, Michigan, where I do a great deal of my hunting. There's an area with a bunch of overgrown Christmas trees and a ridge above it that funnels down into an area we call the Skinner Swamp. On this particular day, I was hunting the area for a monster buck that I had been scouting since early summer. I'd racked up several hours of watching this deer, so I felt like I knew him *and* the places he liked to frequent, inside and out.

The area around Skinner had very little cover, but there was one small patch of thick growth that the buck traveled through a lot—the trees in that patch had rubbed spots all over them from his antlers. This buck's tracks were very identifiable, and today the tracks told me that he was a few hundred yards south of that patch, chasing a doe through a small stretch of land that runs alongside a lake.

I was following the buck's trail when I saw that he'd turned north with the doe. I had an immediate flash of intuition: he was going to cut across the road at Skinner Swamp, then go into that overgrown patch to work his way through the funnel. I formed my strategy in a heartbeat. As soon as that deer headed into the trees, I needed to run full speed into the other end of the overgrowth, get myself into position at least three hundred yards north of where I thought he'd be, get on one knee, dig myself in, and trust that he would come to me.

When the buck entered the trees, I ran as fast I could and worked my way around, using the wind direction to my advantage. I got in position and crawled up next to an old downed tree that was right in the path I was certain he'd take. I knew that buck wasn't going to try to leap over the tree. He'd cut left—and I'd be waiting. I sat down where I could draw clean, took the quiver off my bow, and had just looked up when I heard the buck crashing toward me. He was right on that doe's tail, moving into such thick undergrowth that he couldn't possibly run. Just as I predicted, this beautiful buck walked right in front of me, and with him twelve yards away and looking straight at me, I released the arrow.

How did I do it? I was leveraging Hunter's Wisdom, which involves three types of understanding:

- **Oneness with your prey:** First, we're both animals, and I know the primal triggers that drive any animal's nature—food, sex, survival. I also have a pretty deep understanding of deer in general, and I knew so much about this particular deer that I felt like I was looking at the world through his eyes.

- **Observation-based strategy:** Second, I was able to use all of the data I'd gathered about my prey to form a winning strategy. As soon as that buck made the turn in the general direction of cover, I knew that I had to get down there fast and into position to take him when he arrived.

- **Intuition and anticipation:** Finally, I knew how the story was going to end. I was able to use my instincts to anticipate his moves in those final moments and to act without any hesitation or doubt. I willed that kill through a combination of data, strategy, and intuition.

That's Hunter's Wisdom in action, and you can use the same kind of understanding to score wins in every type of hunt you take on. By walking in others' skin, using that insight to inform a data-based strategy, and then leveraging observation and intuition to anticipate next moves as you implement your strategy, you can take down the biggest, wiliest, most mature targets, no matter how many times they've escaped you in the past. Hunter's Wisdom is one of the most lethal types of leverage you can master in The Hunt.

Becoming One with Your Prey

We live in a culture that prizes individuality, but for hunters, the ability to achieve oneness with others is actually a lot more valuable. That's not as difficult to do as it sounds. First of all, we may have a different type of ego, consciousness, and thought process from other animals, but we're all still animals. Eating, sleeping, mating are pretty much the main activities of hunter and hunted alike. And the aspects of our nature we all share make getting inside another human being's head even easier. The more clearly you understand that you aren't that different from the other animals you work, compete, or live with, the more likely you are to find the strategies and to make the gut calls that will move events toward your Desired Outcomes. That's leverage in action.

The first step in working a Hunter's Wisdom is to put yourself into the mind-set of the animal you're hunting with (or for). Becoming one with the animals in your hunt enables you to answer critical questions like these:

- What do they see and how do they respond to the world around them?
- What does this person want to get out of this hunt?
- How do I appear in their world view? Am I potentially a powerful ally? Am I a threat? Or have they failed to see me at all?
- What is more important to this individual or organization? Their opportunity to score a short-term win? The long-term consequences of this hunt?

Believe it or not, you don't necessarily have to *like* someone to put yourself in their shoes. I once consulted with a company that was having real problems dealing with a showdown between its COO and one of its frontline managers. When I met with each party to the conflict, I heard two entirely different versions of the events that had triggered it. Whereas the COO felt that the manager had demonstrated a stubborn refusal to cooperate, the manager had perceived a lack of clear vision and guidance on the part of the COO. The parties were in agreement about one thing: they'd reached the breaking point.

I pulled the two together and walked through specific examples of how their views differed. By helping them see the problems through *each other's eyes*—and by steering them away from defensiveness or blame—I was able to help them realize that much of their conflict was simply the result of their very different personalities and perspectives. As soon as they acknowledged the obvious contrast in the lenses through which they viewed the world, both were able to look *beyond* those differences to focus on the common ground of DOs they both were targeting. Although they've had to do ongoing maintenance to keep their alliance intact, they've now directed their energy toward hitting company targets rather than toward proving each other wrong.

In business, you have to see the world through the eyes of the person sitting across the table from you, no matter who they are or what they do. When you start by acknowledging how *alike* we all are, you're in a much better position to identify the things that make any individual unique. And remember to keep the Judge out of the process. Seeing the world through someone else's eyes is a lot easier without your ego in the way. When we can develop an understanding of the authentic nature of the animal we're dealing with—whether it's a monster buck, a killer competitor, a critical client, or a much-loved family member—we can leverage that understanding in the hunt ahead.

Tightening Your Strategy

An inexperienced or lazy hunter relies on luck to take an animal, but super-predators rely on their Hunter's Wisdom to build a strategy that maximizes their leverage. Their strategy positions them at the right place and time, and then they strike. When you're able to combine your ability to get into the head of the animal you're hunting, along with leveraging the data points gained through close observation, you'll earn all of the luck you need to take any target.

On a micro level, your strategy is guided by the essential nature you share with your target. On a macro level, you have to cover the target's variables. So, for example, if you're hunting whitetails, you know the main thoroughfares or runways that the deer have been traveling on. You know where they're going to eat in the morning, and where they're returning to sleep after they've finished. You know where they go in the evenings, and when and how they'll get there. By covering the variables, you ground your strategy in evidence.

Of course, an observation-based strategy starts with clearly defined desired outcomes. With your goal clearly fixed, you can do the kind of ego-free observation that pulls in the data points you need to craft a strategy that maximizes opportunities. This is how you increase power through leverage.

As a hunter, my scouting and strategy are shaped by the seasons and cycles of my prey. Because I began using that seasonal approach to strategy back when I was just a kid, it was natural for me to apply the same approach to scouting and strategizing in my businesses. Just about every business has its own cycle, based on seasonal customer needs, organizational buying patterns, grant awards, funding commitments, or whatever. To be able to leverage the variables of a customer, partner, competitor, or client, you need to adapt your scouting and strategy to those cycles. Here's what I mean:

- **Off-season:** You can't do your best deer scouting in the middle of hunting season, so off-season is the best time to take care of a lot of essential groundwork. This is when you should be scouting out trails, placing trail cams, checking your stands, spending time in the areas you *intend* to hunt so you're familiar with the terrain and the animals that live in it. These "seasonal lulls" in business are a good time to attend local events, industry open houses, professional conferences, and so on. These gatherings provide opportunities for you to spot one or two prime targets that you may want to go after. Stay low, though; you don't want to draw their attention *quite* yet.

- **Early season:** This is when the deer population is up; they're starting to feed more heavily and move around more, building up their body mass and strength for the demands that are coming. As a hunter, I use this time to learn about the deer's feeding, movement, and bedding patterns; in other words, I begin to use my off-season observations to construct a strategy. As buying season gets closer in business, I use this time to work hard on retaining clients we already have, growing their business if possible, and identifying the low-hanging fruit in my marketplace. I also do some scouting for new clients and get my name and information out in front of them. I'm not pushing my deals or services; that'll come next. For now, we just want people to know who we are.

• **Pre-rut:** This is the period in hunting when the action starts to heat up. The does aren't quite ready to breed, and the bucks are building up a lot of sexual frustration. I'm scouting and logging data like mad during this time, watching to see what animal is where at what time of day doing what kind of activity. Anything out of the ordinary draws my attention, and I log that, too. This is the time of season when you need to tighten, update, and expand your strategy to prepare it for the hunt ahead. The prebuying season in your industry is *your* selling season—the time when you want to throw all your best stuff out there to draw in buyers. Like those keyed-up bucks, your buyers are looking for a reason to jump. You act as the most successful predator now by becoming the most attractive prey.

- **Rut:** For a bow hunter, this is *Wild Kingdom* time. The animals are running everywhere, chasing each other all over the woods, going crazy with the thrill of mating and fighting and mating some more. The rut's a tricky time to bow hunt—and buying season for any business is just as tricky. It's not easy luring in a government office that's already hot and heavy with another contractor, and you'll have a hard time scoring an advertiser that's already locked into a buy with another media outlet. And if you haven't sold your products or services before buying season begins, you're in trouble.

- **Postseason:** When the rut is over, I take some time to review the results of the season while events are still fresh in my mind. I don't have to worry about going in and scaring animals, so I can do some groundwork, check trails, and see how patterns have changed over the year, looking for any physical signs of unusual activity or events that can teach me something new. I do the same postseason review of my businesses—what have we done that worked? Where did we fall short? What big opportunities have we begun to wedge open for the next season? How can we stop ourselves from making the same mistakes twice? The postseason is an important time to regroup, review, and get ready so that we're well-armed when early-season scouting begins.

Of course, when you're gathering data on a competitor you need to take down or a company you want to partner with, you have to understand more than your target's business cycles and seasons. That in-depth data comes from careful groundwork. You have to know how that individual entity performs in its marketplace—who guides its decisions, where it gets its strength, where its weakest elements are hiding, what types of ideas they've been driven by in the past, and where they've hit their biggest obstacles. And whether you're gathering data on a buck or a business, you have to stay in the background, so that your target doesn't know you're watching. The minute you become part of your target's story, the variables shift. You're no longer observing; you're influencing. Tackle this phase of scouting like a hunter, and you'll find that you're uncovering more data that you can use.

Observation-based strategies are grounded in evidence. That hard-core reality, along with your hunter's experience and intuition, allows you to consider your strategy's details carefully and uncover any weaknesses—which typically occur where you've allowed emotion ("We've always done it this way") or ego ("That's not my problem") to override your Hunter's Wisdom. It's important that you do a really tight review of your plan by thoroughly vetting the details, the way you would any major decision. Unvetted strategies are losing propositions, more likely to damage your prospects for success than to aid them. You can avoid that kind of self-inflicted wound by staying clear, maintaining a neutral mind-set, and targeting every action toward your DOs.

Then, instead of relying on old information, common wisdom, or "what you've always done," scout out your data and put it to work with your primal understanding and intuition to create a strategy that works on *this* day, to take *this* target. Follow that path, and you won't miss too many of the opportunities for leverage that wait for you along the way.

Keeping a Leverage Log

Back in Chapter One, I described an exercise I learned years ago to help me learn to think and live in a more present state—a simple fifteen-minute review of daily events. That kind of replay can help you identify and track your use of leverage points, your performance patterns, and more. But when you're using that reflection to learn more about how you use leverage, your ability to recall may need a boost. I recommend that you use a notebook, or your daily appointment calendar, to track your leverage experiences every hour of the day for two weeks. Whatever form you use

1. If you spot a leverage point, note it.
2. Note every leverage point you use and do a short sketch to map out how you acquired it and what others it opened up for you.
3. If you serve as a leverage point for someone else, note that, too.
4. If you see a place in the trail ahead where you need to strengthen your leverage capabilities, note it, along with any possible options.

Keeping this kind of a log will take a bit of time, but the payoff is huge. You can look for patterns, cycles, clues to your nature that can help you put together a killer strategy for leveraging every skill, asset, connection—even "soft spots"—in your arsenal.

Willing the Win

Any hunt will require that you call on one other aspect of Hunter's Wisdom to take your target: your ability to anticipate your target's actions. Yes, a big part of that ability is built into your strategy and based on data. But True Hunters also rely on their intuition to know how to act and react without conscious reasoning. That's why *intuition* and *visualization* are key elements of leverage in The Hunt.

I'm betting that from the time you were a kid you had moments where you felt like you knew what was going to happen before it began. Some people view intuition as a foggy, feel-good idea, no more than lucky hunches with little basis in reality. But as a hunter, I rely on my intuition. I know that it comes from my instincts and inherent nature—as a super-predator, a human being, a man—and it's fed by experience and *observation*. That last point is crucial, because relying on intuition alone can take us down the trail of fear and paranoia. But when you arm intuition with data, you have a powerful set of tools for decision making at your disposal.

In the real estate business, you won't make it if you can't anticipate growth, so you know in advance where the need for new development will crop up. When I first started in the business, there were no electronic VA (Void Analysis) programs to tell you, down to the inch, where you should spot your new locations. You had to watch what retail players were doing, go to conferences like the International Shopping Center Convention, and talk to experts about what was happening around your state or in any area in which you were planning a move. After doing that for a number of years, I eventually developed a feel for projecting growth areas. I had hard data to go on, too, and my competitors had most of the same intel. But I also had my instincts and intuition telling me what was going to happen next—guidance to which nobody else had access. I was used to leveraging my intuition as a hunter in the field, so it was only natural that I'd work it in my professional life, too. And that leverage helped make me very successful in both kinds of hunting.

When you start exercising your intuition, you'll discover that your brain has logged lots of data that you're not even aware of, and it feeds it to you without any conscious request. You will learn to stop and listen to your gut instead of shooting from the hip. You won't ignore facts, the world around you, or logic and reasoning. In fact, your consciousness pulls all of that data into your memory bank. But you will be open to wisdom that reaches further and deeper than any of that—wisdom based just as firmly on reality, yet not visually or physically available at your fingertips. Your intuition, along with your strategic and elemental understanding of your prey, will help you automatically size up the signs and determine your target's next move. And it allows you to pivot on a dime when you need to.

The best way to hone your intuition is by listening to it, testing it, and having confidence in it. Over the years, I've learned to ride my intuition like a motorcycle, bobbing and weaving around obstacles, speeding through clear territory, and zipping into tight places that I might not have been able to access with the heavier gear of conscious reasoning. You can do that, too, and you'll be amazed at the results.

You must be able to trust your intuition. When I'm preparing to carry out a strategy in any hunt, I fully believe that I'm going to land the trophy I'm aiming for. I don't walk into the woods with a "Gosh, I really hope I take that deer" attitude. I know I'm prepared to take the prize, because I have all the pieces of the puzzle before me. And over the years I've learned that the final step in implementing my strategy is to hunt with a full-on belief that wills the win to happen.

There's nothing supernatural or psychic about leveraging your intuition to anticipate the next moves of those you live and work with. It's a skill that you can develop, based on tools you're born with—your senses, your brain, and your ability to think things through, connect the dots, and project data from past experiences into future events. Like a lot of the techniques we've talked about in this book, beefing up your intuition and using it to anticipate next moves really is just a practice. When you're evaluating a client or competitor, or deciding how to advance an alliance or relationship, do a gut check. Ask yourself how you think the story is going to develop, based on everything you know and feel about the situation. Make the call, leverage your hunter's intuition, and then act on it with conviction. Don't be tentative. Trust your gut to help you stay one step ahead of whatever you're hunting for.

Building a Jet Stream

The world is full of leverage points for True Hunters; some will work with your values and needs, others won't. The more practice you have in the leverage of The Hunt, the better you'll be at spotting and using what works. Then you can leave behind the shiny objects that don't play any useful function in your hunt. And the more you use leverage points—people, events, issues, chance meetings, weather changes, you name it—the faster you'll move, and the more new ones you'll spot. That's how you create what I call a *Leverage Jet Stream*. When you have the power of that jet stream with you, you can fly. Your hunt gets stronger, your targets get bigger, and the possibilities in front of you are limitless.

A Leverage Jet Stream is an amazing pathway to rapid success that's available to just about anyone. Simply put, when you have a developed network of connections— including people, resources, events, ideas—that network becomes a power source that continues to pull in *more* opportunity and build *more* power. The more you understand the Leverage Jet Stream's efficiency, the better you'll be able to use it. For example, technological advancements and globalization are creating new niche industries all the time, in everything from antique violin restoration to medical tourism management to plant-based alternative energy development. If you're working in a niche industry, you very likely have some contact with just about every person, area, and element of that niche. Now think about how all of those elements are connected to each other and how all of them connect back to you. By visualizing those connections, you're positioning yourself to build a jet stream in that niche that will offer you the fastest possible path forward. Then you can put together a strategy that will set your Leverage Jet Stream in motion.

Leverage Jet Streams don't have to be complex to bring great results. When I was in real estate, I once sat on a board with the president of a local college. He talked to me about his organization's vision, which involved expanding the campus and its facilities. Weeks later, I was contacted by a local school district that wanted to relocate its administrative offices but first needed to sell its current location—which was adjacent to my fellow board member's college campus. I was scheduled to give a talk the following day to community leaders about strategies for maximizing the value of real estate holdings, and I was pretty sure the college president would be there. When I saw him in the audience, I made sure to emphasize the importance of owning real estate adjacent to core operations, and I included specific examples involving academic and medical campuses. I approached the president after my talk and told him about my client's interest in selling the real estate directly connected to his campus. The deal brought me a commission, and it established a working relationship between my firm and both academic organizations that led to multiple offshoot deals down the road. That simple confluence of client, contacts, and opportunities is a perfect illustration of a Leverage Jet Stream in action.

Lots of people have the makings of a Leverage Jet Stream. However, they can't figure out how to get it moving, or they need to be better at navigating as it picks up speed. The techniques and approaches you're learning in this book will help you build that bridge over those obstacles. First, you need to know where you want this jet stream to take you. When you've achieved complete clarity about your Desired Outcome, you can continue to use consciousness to see your situation, the ecosystem in which you're hunting, all of its elements, and the connections that link them together. After that, your authenticity will help you find the leverage points within those connections that fit with your goals and values and move you toward your target. With that strategy in place, you can begin to execute, using your leverage points wisely, moving quickly and effectively toward your DOs, pivoting when necessary—but always staying on track. When you do this, your Leverage Jet Stream begins to grow.

Sometimes, mapping your leverage points can help you jumpstart your Leverage Jet Stream. Begin by drawing a visual diagram of one of your current desired outcomes and the people, events, locations, and issues that surround it. Next, map the connections among those elements, to form the most direct and effective path toward the goal you've listed on the diagram. If you have trouble with this exercise, start by identifying one experience in which you recognized a connection point with some other person, place, event, or issue in your industry or territory and then were able to leverage that connection to advance toward your desired outcome. Diagram that experience by connecting the leverage elements you used to the outcome you achieved. The practice of identifying leverage points and then visually charting their connections to a success is a great way to begin honing your leveraging instincts.

Your Leverage Jet Stream will continue to become bigger and more powerful over time, but only if you remember one critical truth: if you want to tap into the other sources out there, you must be *a source of leverage yourself.* You can't dismiss people when they come to you for a boost in building their own Leverage Jet Stream. In fact, you bulk up your own leverage power by offering your leverage to others whenever you can. You give, and you get, and that's how the world goes around. No one succeeds alone. We all need to leverage the power of other people, other organizations, other systems, just as we need the good luck that comes to all able navigators.

One Man's Ride on the Leverage Jet Stream

Jim Schiefelbein is an incredible guy; he's an avid hunter, CEO, entrepreneur, and an outstanding example of the power of leverage. In 1996, Jim quit his job as a service writer at Toyota, and he and his wife sold off their assets and moved to the little town of Ottawa, Illinois. Their house had a four-car garage, and Jim's dad, a retailer, saw a good use for that space. He'd recently begun buying printer toner cartridges from a guy who was building them in his garage, and he told Jim the business looked simple and lucrative. Jim did some scouting and saw his opportunity. The printer supply industry was in its infancy stages—no after-market support, nothing but expensive OEM brands available. Leveraging his remaining assets and every credit card he had, Jim started Clover Technologies and began building toner cartridges in his own garage. Through trial and error, he came up with some unique manufacturing solutions and soon had staked a claim in the marketplace, offering high quality at a killer cost. Now he needed another round of leverage to grow the business.

Jim turned to the Small Business Administration for help. "I took advantage of community development assistance programs," he told me, "to buy and sell things to create equity, so I could build credibility to get some loans." Then Jim built and leveraged strong relationships within his industry. "I robbed Peter to pay Paul and worked closely with vendors and customers," he said. "I had great relationships with both sides, and I communicated with them very well along the way."

When Jim landed office-supply giant Staples as a client, his business jumped to $6 million in sales very quickly—and he had an account that was going to require a lot of capital. To power up his Leverage Jet Stream even further, Jim formed an alliance with a customer-turned-friend who was looking to get into a new business.

"He was really familiar with our business and our industry. I brought him in for some equity, and that's when we took on some bank financing. Then it really started to jump." By 2001, Clover Technologies made *Inc.* magazine's list of the Top 500 Fastest-Growing Private Companies, and it remained on that list for the next three years running.[2]

As the business grew to $50 million, then $100 million in sales, Jim knew he had to leverage different kinds of expertise and opportunity. "We hired an investment bank, and I really got my feet wet in private equity." Keeping his eye on the core business, Jim began to diversify Clover Technologies, "from recycling to remanufacturing to electronics manufacturing to any kind of other remanufacturing component in that business model." He explained, "We added layers of management and created the tools we needed to make the business effective. When you're growing like that, you're not necessarily efficient at all. But then you grab your leaders in around you, you communicate your message, and you make sure they're always around everything that's going on."

Jim's relentless leveraging paid off. When he sold the company in 2004, Clover had grown from a one-man, garage-based business to a company with customers on five continents and over $300 million in sales. As of this writing, the company's at $1 billion in sales and still growing—a rapid rise to success that was launched through the leverage of a True Hunter!

Getting to the Gatekeepers

Everyone talks about networking, but not all that many people are really *good* at it. A lot of networking failures are really just the fault of an ego that got in the way. Leverage is about getting into the right space, but you have to get next to the gatekeeper before you can get through to the other side of the gate. Instead of running up and banging on the door of whatever king-maker you want to leverage, you need to outline your best path forward. The process is similar to others in The Hunt:

1. Define your problem.
2. Define the Desired Outcome.
3. Identify the layers of contacts you'll need to leverage to get to that DO.
   Tier 1—The Direct Source
   Tier 2—Those who work or live immediately with or are close to the Direct Source
   Tier 3—Those who work or live with or know Tier 2 people
   Tier 4—Those who work or live with or know Tier 3 people, and so on

Depending how big a dog you're chasing, you may have to work your way through even more tiers to get access to him or her. Let's say you've created a line of products decorated with the University of Michigan logo, and you want the university to help market those products. Your DO is to get to and leverage the person at the university who can okay U of M's involvement:

1. **Tier 1**, the Direct Source—in this case it's the university's logoed product buyer.

2. **Tier 2** contacts could be people who own the shops who sell the university's products, companies that manufacture NCAA products, and so on.
3. **Tier 3** contacts could be people who work in those Tier 2 organizations, who have access to actual customer knowledge, and who are directly involved in selling U of M logoed products.
4. **Tier 4** contacts could be high-ranking U of M alumni who buy logoed products (or people who know them), or who have connections to one of the university's coaches, top team members, or athletic program managers.

The more groundwork you do, and the better your scouting, the more people you'll find to fit these tiers, and the more tiers you'll uncover. *Tiered leverage* is crucial. If you can get Tier 2 or 3 to love and endorse what you are trying get done, you'll immediately take on more credibility with Tier 1. And, always, the most desirable leverage position you can be in is a win-win situation. You'll get the most leverage in your hunt from the person who stands the most to gain by giving it to you.

That's the most important thing to remember about leveraging your way up. All along the way, people are going to want to know how they can benefit from helping you. "If I help you score a meeting with CEO X, what benefits will *I* get from any relationship that develops?"

Then, when you're able to pull a power player into your corner, everyone else will come sniffing around, wanting to know how you took the trophy and how they can share in your prize. "Who is this guy? Should we be doing business with him?" You can't be sidetracked by those kinds of distractions. Your challenge is to find and leverage the gatekeepers—the people who can walk you through the door and move you closer and closer to the big dog you need to win over.

In the summer of 2011, I wanted to expand OHub's model into agriculture—an initiative I called AgHub. I was able to leverage the jet stream of advertising agency connections we'd formed at OHub, many of which represented advertising brands in the agricultural world. We also leveraged opportunities with some of our outdoor clients that had advertising budgets available for playing in the ag world—budgets to which we'd never before had access.

OutdoorHub had the technology and tools behind us to stake a claim in this new market. But to really move our model into prime territory, I had to have an incredibly strong marketing and sales team. I hired the best agriculture sales exec in the country, and I convinced him to join us by leveraging the success we'd already built online. That guy knew all of the best sales reps working in the ag world today, and he went out and brought some of them in to build our team. And with that sales group in our corner, we had our gatekeeper—really, a team of gatekeepers. Through them, we were able to get in front of some of the biggest advertisers in the U.S. agricultural market. I worked my way through the tiers and landed the big dogs I needed to establish my proven model in a new market.

Getting through the gate won't help you, though, if you don't stay smart and use your leverage wisely. That sounds like basic info, but planning your pursuit of a Tier 1 contact isn't always easy. Let's say you've got a meeting with someone who really carries some weight in the territory you want to hunt. You're not sure how you want to leverage this connection, but you're certain that building a relationship with this person could bring you endless opportunities. You're already familiar with the answer here: You have to fall back on your DOs.

Go into that meeting with one or two Desired Outcomes clear in your mind. They don't have to be your *ultimate* outcomes, just clear problems or questions or results that you want this person to help you answer or achieve. Because your time will be limited, you need to plan the presentation of your DOs accordingly. If your meeting is scheduled for an hour, plan on spending no more than twenty minutes on your DOs. Then go into the meeting with a neutral mind, willing to go with the direction the conversation takes you. You want to see and retain as much as you can, and to be flexible enough to spot opportunities that you hadn't expected to find. Finally, remember to *shut up* and *listen*. To help keep that in mind, I write the letters "SUL" at the top of any DO list I take into meetings that could offer important leverage opportunities.

Of course, all of this advice is just one piece of the bigger process of leverage that we've been talking about throughout this chapter. Whether you're leveraging your time with the owner of a major corporation or one of the guys who cleans the cafeteria there, remember these basics:

- Leverage your inherent nature.
- Leverage the things you understand and share with the person you're dealing with.
- Time your leveraging opportunities carefully.
- Don't let your ego blind you to the opportunities you hadn't planned for.

We all have access to a whole herd of leverage points, but not everyone is able to spot or use them. Even the biggest opportunity is only as good as the knowledge and skill of the hunter who leverages it.

Building a Bigger Muscle

Because it's such a critical skill, leverage really should be as instinctual to you as breathing. In fact, it's an act of success *and* survival. If you overlook, ignore, or refuse to leverage an opportunity, you're wasting the time and effort you've invested in every other aspect of your hunt for success.

But no matter how weak you might think your leveraging muscles have become, you *can* get them back in shape. You just have to wake up your instincts and put the skills and techniques we've talked about in this chapter into practice. Racers train for the race, weightlifters train for the trials, and you have to train for The Hunt. Leverage is just one of the muscles you'll need to hit your target—but it's one you can't do without. So it's worth the work it takes to develop it.

I know how it is; you look around at your über-social friends or at other people in your office, schmoozing the crowd, working the room, looking like they were born with some kind of supernatural gift for getting what they want out of every situation that comes their way. And yes, some people *are* more skillful than others at spotting and using opportunity. So what does that have to do with you? Get above your ego, True Hunter, and survey this situation for what it really is. You aren't limited by someone else's success. Instead, you need to find a way to *leverage* it. What can you learn from all of those schmoozers? Could you leverage what or who they know to start your own Leverage Jet Stream? Where have you seen them tank, and what can you learn from that? Whatever you might think, very few of them are killing all the time—and you can learn as much from their misses as you can from their hits.

Most important, don't get caught in a swamp of fear and negative expectations. Be clear, and be real. With practice, you'll get better at recognizing available opportunities and choosing the strongest and most effective options among them. Then it's just a matter of acting with purpose and courage—remaining on target as you uncover and use new opportunities, assessing your own value as a leverage point for others, and networking relentlessly. That's how you build your leverage muscle, and that's how you push through and find the wins.

Remember: nobody makes it alone in this world. The day you stop using your leverage is the day you drop out of The Hunt.

The Last Thirty Minutes of Daylight

Leverage is the power that keeps life moving. Take these ideas about leverage with you on every hunt:

- **All animals survive by leveraging opportunity.** The better you are at leverage, the more successful you'll be on any hunt.
- **Leveraging one opportunity always creates more opportunity.** Like a row of dominos, one successful leveraging moment often triggers the next, which triggers the next, and on it goes.
- **Know your nature clearly**, and leverage every aspect of it. When it comes to leverage, everything can be an opportunity, so understand and use both your strengths *and* your weaknesses.

- **Every animal has a natural cycle.** The more you know about your own patterns, the better you'll be at using that cycle to improve your performance.

- **Scout your daily work habits to determine your Peak Activity Window.** Block out those hours, protect them from all interruption, and use them to do the most mentally demanding work on your plate.

- **Your time and energy are the most valuable commodities you control.** Don't waste them—and guard them against waste by others.

- **Use your Hunter's Wisdom.** Identify with your prey, create an observation-based strategy, and anticipate next moves. Then hunt with conviction.

- **Identify every element in your ecosystem that can be leveraged.** Then track the connections that link those elements to build a Leverage Jet Stream.

- **Use tiered leverage** to get to and through the gatekeepers that will give you access to the top dogs.

- **Shut up and listen.** Go into meetings with upper-level connections with two questions or problems that you want this person to discuss with you; then let the conversation develop naturally.

BRINGING IT HOME:
REAL-TIME EXECUTION

Have you ever seen film footage of a cheetah taking down a gazelle? The big cat crouches low as it stalks through tall grass to get close to the herd, then locks on a target as the animals bolt for their lives. The cheetah dodges rocks, leaps over fallen trees, and weaves through undergrowth, to stay close on the heels of its targeted prey. If that animal moves out of range, the cheetah adjusts course in mid-stride to go after another that represents a more likely target.

Every act and instinct in the cheetah's hunt is directed toward one goal: capturing food for survival. That's *real-time execution*—the kind of seamless, agile, and intensely focused pursuit that brings home the goods for any hunter. Real-time execution can move you through hazards, around obstacles, and on toward whatever targeted outcome brings you success.

You don't have to go to the African savannah to see real-time execution at work. Individuals, organizations, even governments have to be strong, flexible, and tightly focused to take down their own targets in a world that changes rapidly and is unforgiving of failure. Peyton Manning, who I think may be the best quarterback in NFL history, is a master of real-time execution. Manning seems to see the whole field and every player on it as his territory. His DO is to win the game, to do whatever it takes to move the ball down the field and score points: making decisions in real time, calling an audible on the fly, exploiting the best available resources, and pivoting to take every available advantage.

In the process of navigating my company around the obstacles I'd thrown in my own path with the WHA launch and then on through the hazards of months that followed, I certainly had to become a master of real-time execution, too. It was a process that helped me fully understand the essential role of this fourth pillar of The Hunt.

Getting the DC lobbyists off my back hadn't been enough to save my business. My startup cash was running out, and I was struggling to find a way to bring the WHA back to life. One day, while deep in meditation, I had a breakthrough idea. I didn't have to continue fighting my way through this swamp; I could *change direction*.

So I began scouting a new path. I went online and researched the places where advertisers were spending money—like the websites of *Field and Stream* and *Outdoor Life*—along with the sites my attackers had used as their weapons to go after the WHA. I also dug into the ad agencies' own sites—and immediately saw an opportunity. If I became the aggregator that brought all of that online ad space together in one package, I could build a valuable business—fast. I knew that business would make way more sense than the original tournament idea for hitting my ultimate goals of (1) making money for my investors while (2) bringing more mainstream attention to the outdoor industry and the sport of hunting.

In a heartbeat, the WHA was dead—and OutdoorHub was born. I restaffed my business and began reviewing every phase of the existing online advertising model to find ways to bump up our profit margins. Then I scheduled a meeting with my investors. The rapid pivots I'd made with the business had shaken their confidence in me. But when I promised that the business would be profitable within ten months of our meeting—by October of 2007—they calmed down and left me to live up to my word. That solid date gave my investors a concrete metric for my on-the-fly execution.

I got to work immediately, aggregating the combined traffic and reach of a large number of previously fragmented sites. To maximize that network's profitability, I moved away from the traditional revenue-sharing model to a fixed-rate model that bumped our profits by another

30 percent. Now I had to start selling through the ad space. I began by offering big-name advertisers ninety days of free advertising with the deal that if they were satisfied they would put me on a buy for the next quarter; they agreed. After landing that first collection of big fish, I went after the next-biggest, who were happy to jump in, too. With that, I was halfway to my goal of profitability.

I doubled down on my efforts, leveraging a contact from college who worked with GM. He saw the value we brought to the table and agreed to do a three-month test. The test run was so successful that Chevy agreed to a monthly ad buy, which hiked OHub's profitability right up where I'd promised my investors it would be, and right on time. After that, there was no looking back.

I still had plenty of challenges ahead, but I'd hit my target—and the partnership between GM and OutdoorHub remains mutually beneficial to this day. I achieved that success through real-time execution, the same kind of powerful hunting technique a cheetah uses to take down its prey.

In The Hunt method, real-time execution involves these specific elements:

1. Targeting and tracking *real* data in a crowded, fast-moving field
2. Pivoting on-the-fly to adjust your tactics, change techniques, or go after a more effective or efficient target

3. Developing real-time strategies to move into new territory
4. Knowing when to stick it out and when to walk away
5. Closing the hunt with the same intense focus that launched it

Sometimes, making a very powerful shift is a simple maneuver. A slight shift in the trail can be easy to miss as you go forward yet seem incredibly obvious in the rear-view mirror. Making successful on-the-fly pivots is what real-time execution is all about. When you train yourself to operate with real-time execution, you're positioned to spot—and act on—the small but mighty opportunities that lie hidden all around you.

And, believe me, they're there. Some of the greatest innovations in the world are less about radical invention and more about tiny but ingenious tweaks that make all the difference. Take Facebook; that global game-changer was really a slight alteration to the now largely forgotten MySpace model. Or consider Amazon—simply an online version of a massive retail catalog. Remember when Entertainment Book or Valpak almost exclusively dominated the coupon world? Groupon is just an online version of the traditional coupon-book idea. The list of market-revolutionizing tweaks goes on and on. Real-time execution—in combination with other pillars of The Hunt—helps you recognize even the most well-camouflaged opportunities that cross your path and then make the on-the-fly pivots necessary to leverage them. And finding the right tweaks can make all the difference in your outcomes.

Real-time execution requires that you remain present and focused on finding the best way forward instead of sticking with an ineffective plan. It means allowing yourself to be guided by faith in your skills, your process, and your ability to make the best call and then act on it. Real-time execution is a key weapon of any great hunter and every great business leader, and it's a critical element of The Hunt method. From launching the pursuit of a Desired Outcome, to taking the shot that makes that trophy yours, when you bring the skills of real-time execution to your hunt, you exponentially increase your chances for realizing exceptional results.

Targeting and Tracking

Identifying your Desired Outcomes means that you must *really* understand the ultimate goal you're shooting for, because you may have to shift directions rapidly as you make progress toward that outcome. When you go after what you want with intensity, you have to be both nimble *and* focused. You have faith in your process, but at the same time you're being guided by real-time events and opportunities.

To execute change fluidly, you need to have the data necessary to trust what's happening as it happens and make the right calls as your strategy develops. That data will fit into two categories:

- **Macro data**—big-picture information, based for the most part on research
- **Micro data**—the more detailed information you gather from personal observation

So, let's say that I'm getting ready for a November hunt in Kansas. I'll look at macro data to determine whether a hunt there will be worth the trip. I'll assess seasonal weather patterns and recent reports and see what other hunters in the area have said about the rut. This macro data is important in business for the same reasons. Knowing what the other players in your market are doing and what overall economic trends or world events are influencing the field allows you to determine whether you're interested in moving into that territory—or taking off in another direction entirely.

When the macro data checks out, you can begin pulling in your micro data. In Kansas, I'll scout out the best ranges to hunt, the best places to locate my stand. I'll look at what's going on in the woods. Do I see bucks chasing does? Do I hear them grunting? Can I hear young fawns bleating because their moms left them alone to go off with a buck? That's the kind of micro data that lets me know breeding season has kicked in and this spot is hot.

You'll have to do the same kind of on-the-ground tracking to turn up the micro data you'll need to build a strategy for taking targeted outcomes in your own pursuits.

For example, OHub is in the internet business, which means that if I want to build out a strategy for growing its business, I need to track the internet and media markets. Is TV up this year, or down? Is video pre-roll ad space up or down? Is display advertising hot? At a macro level, these kinds of questions help me determine where big advertisers will focus, so I can be certain that we're going to deliver products that meet that market's demands. Think of this phase as that time when the cheetah stalks through the tall grass, eyeing the herd and choosing his target.

Then I break it down to the micro data. What are my direct competitors offering? What are people buying from them—and what are they ignoring? By visiting the websites of OHub's competitors and their customers, I can begin to piece together the strategies top competitors are using. Then I drill down deeper, identifying flaws and looking for ways I can exploit them. By tracking what the industry is doing on a macro level, and what my competitors are doing on a micro level, I can pull together my own strategy for taking down the DOs I've identified for the year.

We've talked about scouting multiple times in this book, so I don't need to rehash the details of that process here. Just remember that you'll never be able to hunt with real-time execution if you don't carefully target your DOs and track down the data necessary to take those big wins. Events can change in a heartbeat. And your research gives you the muscles and flexibility you'll need to make any fast pivots necessary to stay on the trail of success. That buck I'm tracking in Kansas may get killed by another hunter on the second day of the season. If I'm not out there in the woods, following the trail and taking in data in real time, I could end up hunting a ghost instead of identifying and switching to a new target and moving on to take it. If your focus wavers during your own hunt, if you stop tracking available data, you can find yourself chasing unachievable—or even undesirable—outcomes, too. That's a sure way to fruitlessly exhaust your resources.

Pivoting to Take the Prey You Didn't See Coming

When hunting on our family farm in Michigan, I always used a favorite tree stand. But one year I realized that the deer activity around that stand had dropped off dramatically over the past few seasons. As I studied the area from above, I started thinking that perhaps I was missing deer movement in a dense cluster of cedar trees to the west. So I waited until the deer were down for the night, and then moved my stand over to that area.

The change-up worked. That patch of cedars had grown so thick that it had formed a perfect cover; even from just forty yards away, I couldn't see or hear the deer crossing through it. That small, quick pivot in location became the breakout moment of my hunt. I wrapped up the season by taking a beautiful nine-point buck from that stand, along with an important lesson: I'd chosen my original location after a lot of careful scouting and tracking, and it had worked well for a while. But things change. By rethinking my approach and reconsidering the available data coming to me on the fly—by hunting with real-time execution—I was able to change my approach and score a win that had been escaping me in these woods for the past few years.

The question isn't *whether* you'll have to pivot; it's *when*. No brand, product, message, or approach will carry you forever. And sometimes the biggest opportunities and most lethal competition will come from a person or company or marketplace or material you've never even heard of. Nothing in Blockbuster's business model prepared it to deal with Netflix. Borders wasn't positioned to deal with competition from online booksellers or the technologies that evolved into e-books and iTunes. For these and many other businesses that once ruled their marketplace, a slow response time proved to be fatal. You never know where the most deadly fire will come from, but you can be certain that someone, sometime will have you in their sights. If you aren't agile, you risk being taken down.

Even though you can't predict what new disruption will flip your marketplace, you *can* know your own business model thoroughly and then view it from the elevated perspective of consciousness. That clear, unemotional vision, along with ongoing scouting, tracking, and targeting, will help you identify areas of vulnerability in your operation or approach that represent opportunities for others to jump into or even reshape your own marketplace. You can leverage that intel to build a barrier to your competitors' entry, or to leapfrog over them and lay claim to new territories. When you know which path you need to take forward, you have a big part of the information you'll need for executing the move.

But mighty or mini, fast shift or slow turn, every pivot in the real-time execution of any hunt involves three elements:

1. Making the call
2. Choosing the path
3. Executing the change

Knowing when it's time to pivot is a skill you develop over time. To master any process, though, you have to understand exactly what it involves. So let's look at these steps in more detail.

You know it's time to pivot when you uncover a point of vulnerability in your model. That takes some scouting and reflection. When Netflix saw the growing popularity of video streaming, it had to pivot quickly from its DVD-through-the-mail model and begin offering monthly subscriptions that gave customers instant online access to the films they wanted to see. As voices of concerns about obesity and heart health grew louder in the United States, fast-food franchises like McDonald's and Wendy's pivoted to move beyond the meat-and-potatoes models that built their successes by offering salads and fresh fruit options, and announcing plans to eliminate trans fats from their products. In fact, you have to be watchful and proactive to stay on top of any important hunt. If you want to scout out vulnerabilities in your own business model, you'll need to ask yourself questions like these:

- How do you compare to your competition when it comes to keeping pace with marketplace changes?
- What's your market position? Is your market share growing?
- What are the barriers to entry in your market?
- What do you do better than anyone?
- How easily could a current player in the market morph into something that threatens your position? Who is your biggest threat in this arena?
- How easy would it be for a player from a slightly *different* market to come in and eat your lunch?
- Is there any one customer or factor that could make your model obsolete?
- Is your model flexible enough to account for changing market conditions? Do your margins enable you to

adjust to changes that are out of your control and still stay profitable?

- In order to execute on your model, do you need the participation of talent that could be hard to train and retain? Or do you need talent that's relatively easy to find and/or train?
- Is your model scalable?

When you follow the pillars of The Hunt method, you position yourself to see where your business—or your life—is trending. That can help you determine what path your pivot should take. Then you can make the moves that will put you just far enough in front of that trend to own it. Remember, your goal in executing any change isn't necessarily to be a radical pioneer, leading from so far out in front that you've lost your followers. At OutdoorHub, I made a really radical change of direction through a series of pivots.

Very few of us are successful at making dramatic, game-changing shifts in a heartbeat. If your doctor wants you to lose weight and lower your blood pressure, for example, she probably won't recommend that you leave her office, drive to the nearest gym and do a two-hour workout, then stop at the grocery store on the way home to buy all of the food you'll need to completely revolutionize your diet, beginning with that evening's meal. The biggest rebuilding efforts sometimes have to begin with small, incremental efforts. If you swing in with a wrecking ball, you can damage your infrastructure to the point that it falls apart before you have an opportunity to reshape it to your needs.

You execute this kind of step-by-step shift fluidly by testing every step and every pivot against your Desired Outcomes. What *are* the goals you originally set out to achieve? Are they still valid? Where will you be if you accomplish your DOs? Is that your idea of success? What do you have to do to get there? Sometimes the answers to these questions can lead you to change up your DOs. Other times, you're going to have to tweak—or even transform—your approach, so that you're happy with the model you've put in place. When you have a clear and unemotional vision of the real world—where you are, how you got here, where you want to go, and how you want things to be when you get there—then taking the next steps necessary to build a model that will get you to your goals will be as natural and fluid as a stream flowing into a river.

Being Present to Pivot

In the end, your strongest weapon for pulling off effective pivots is your ability to *be there*. People, ideas, events—the world is constantly firing new information, new roadblocks, new opportunities at you. If you can stay alert to that action, you'll be two steps ahead of the sleepwalking world and ready to pivot toward a better path or jump on an opening.

My brother Andy once asked me to handle a showing with a large tenant that was in the newspaper and print business. While I was walking the team through this building, it became clear to me that they hated the space *and* the location—and given what they were looking for, I didn't disagree with them. I realized that these people were there as a favor to our company, and there was no way they were going to take this space. But I also realized that the CEO of the newspaper agency was one of the people on the tour, and she was in charge of content for the tenant's organization. That gave me an idea for turning a losing afternoon for the real estate business into a positive opportunity for OutdoorHub, where we were just beginning to syndicate content. I scheduled a meeting with the CEO for the following week, and we began working on a syndication deal to make this organization a pilot paper for our content.

If I'd mentally checked out during the showing and merely gone through the motions, the idea for that pivot wouldn't even have shown up on my radar. Initial objective: build a relationship with the tenants in order to lease them some space from Farbman Group. Pivot: build relationship and try to get a content deal done for OutdoorHub.

Simply *being there*—paying attention to body language; listening to and understanding what people are really saying; watching the way people, businesses, marketplaces, even countries interact with each other—doesn't require any kind of superhuman strength or skill. But it's an essential element of understanding when, where, and how to pivot. When you walk through the world with a closed mind, you close off your access to any number of pivot points that can move you further down the road toward your Desired Outcomes. Without those open avenues, you can end up walking into a big mess, when—not if—you have to rethink your way forward.

Moving into New Territory

Most of us spend a lot of time prospecting for new clients, deals, or other business in today's high-pressure environment of heavy hunting and a hard economy. To succeed in that territory, you need to operate in stealth mode— mindful of both your own moves and those around you. Your goal in entering new territory is to get out in front of your targets without letting anyone know you're within range. By the time your quarry senses your presence, you are at full draw with your arrow nocked and aimed straight at their heart. Here's what I mean.

In 2003, Manoj Bhargava sampled a sixteen-ounce energy drink at a natural products trade show in California.[1] Bhargava liked the amped-up energy the drink delivered, and was certain that he could sell it. But he was sure that sixteen ounces wasn't a necessary fit with the product's promise. As he saw it, the drink's strongest selling point was its ability to make you more productive, not less thirsty— so why position it to compete with soft drinks?

So Bhargava began producing his own energy drink in a two-ounce bottle. His team hustled to get it placed near the cash registers of stores like GNC and, in a major score, Walmart. In just eight years, 5-Hour Energy drinks became a billion-dollar business. Bhargava wasn't experienced in making and marketing beverages, but he was a pro at moving into and mastering new territories. From clearing debris from crumbling neighborhoods in Philadelphia, to helping at his family's PVC manufacturing company in Fort Wayne, Indiana, or doing construction on ashrams in India, Bhargava had become a master of execution. His winning development of 5-Hour Energy was no exception; he quickly identified an existing product's strongest selling point and vulnerabilities, and he devised leveragable tweaks that would position his version of the product outside the range of its most threatening competitors. That's the way to use real-time execution to stalk into new territory and start taking trophies.

Let's face it: you enter a new market with the ultimate hope of owning it, and real-time execution is your key in that quest. Whether you're a start-up or an established business trying something new, Step One is to ask yourself the same types of questions you ask at the beginning of any pivot:

- Who are the current players in this field?
- Who's out ahead?

- How solid are they financially, and how strong is their team?
- After looking at all of this data, what unique opportunity do you see to step in and grab market share?
- How do these things coincide with our current strengths, actual capacity, and DOs?

With your targeting and real-time tracking data before you, you can put together your plan for breaking into the market—or not. If you're tracking game, and you find signs that several other hunters have been in an area over the last two weeks, you know that the territory is overly pressured. You have to decide whether your skill level and techniques are going to give you a good chance to go in and succeed in that area, or whether you're just going to be one more unlucky hunter aiming for (and unlikely to take) targets in a crowded space. Remember, True Hunters don't confuse activity with results.

Step Two is to connect the data you've gathered to your current skills and strengths by looking beyond market boundaries and buzzwords and into the ideas and events and people that are shaping the space you want to own.

Once you know the common wisdom of your new market, you can create a plan that disrupts it. Survey your existing business model, skills, ideas, and experiences to find your own unique leverage points. Check your ego and allow yourself to see the connections between your existing tools and the new work that lies ahead. By relating new challenges back to the hunt your team knows, you're better able to execute strongly and fluidly—even on unfamiliar turf.

Claiming Your Space

Kim Brink, VP of Marketing for NASCAR and former director of advertising and sales promotion for Chevrolet and Cadillac, has been on the frontlines in the corporate fight to maintain the authenticity of a strong brand while taking it to a whole new market demographic. But before she could take on any of those targets, Kim had to claim some new territory of her own.

In 1990, Kim was working in the market research department at General Motors. When she tried to move into an open marketing position with Chevrolet, the general marketing manager told her that first she'd have to go to work in a field sales position. When Kim explained that field sales wouldn't work for her, the manager replied, "Then you're never gonna work in marketing at this company."

Kim didn't see that answer as an endpoint. Instead, she landed a job in product planning, work that gave her more face time with GM's designers and engineers— and more opportunity to scout out the signature ideas and core design elements that shaped the company's major brands. Two years later, Kim applied for an ad manager's position in the truck division, where Mac Whisner was managing Chevy's hugely successful "Like a Rock" campaign. Kim's grounding in the company's brand basics got her the job. She'd carved her own path into the territory she wanted to hunt.

The experience served her well. When executives at Chevrolet decided to target a "greener," younger, more urban demographic, Kim's job was to find a way to stake a claim in that new market without driving away the existing customers and advertisers. Knowing that "great brands start with the product and what makes it great," Kim and her colleagues leveraged Chevrolet's strongest crossover elements to create the American Revolution campaign, which succeeded in reaching the old *and* new areas of the company's target demographic.

At Cadillac, Kim faced the same challenge, as the company scrambled to appeal to new blood, for the long-term health of a brand whose customer base, with an average age of seventy, was (literally) dying. "They were going to come out with a new look, a complete product overhaul," Kim told me. "And they needed the marketing to be as bold as the product itself. That's when we conceived of the Led Zeppelin campaign."

Kim took that idea to her boss, Mark LaNeve, who was ready to shake things up. "We forged a partnership to say this is going to work—not being afraid of how senior GM management is going to worry about it, or how the marketplace is going to perceive it." The campaign was launched with what became known as Cadillac's Breakthrough commercial, and it helped bring one of America's most traditional national brands into the focus of a whole new audience.

Kim's experiences are perfect illustrations of the way True Hunters use real-time execution to enter into new territory without sacrificing any of the strengths that have helped them claim past trophies. Whether you're getting ready to carve new space in your personal *or* professional life, the process is the same: Do your groundwork, leverage your strongest weapons, and have confidence in your vision; then you can move fearlessly toward your ultimate goals—no matter what new directions your path takes.

Sitting Out Bad Weather, or Making the Call to Bail

Part of being an experienced hunter is learning when to stick—with the hunt, the location, the technique, the tools—and when to call it quits and move on. I remember clearly one of the more painful lessons I've learned about making those calls. Many years ago, I spent an entire summer scoping out an area around one of my more productive tree stands, and I'd spotted a buck that I was determined to track that autumn. I called him Old Grey. He was monstrously large, easily four and a half years old, and incredibly smart. I'd seen him a few times through my binoculars, and I'd even caught a few trail-cam pics of him, but he never seemed to slip up. I knew that if I was ever going to take him, I'd have to be smarter than he was.

One day, well into the season, I'd been in the tree stand all day waiting for this dude to show up. The wind was howling, stirring up the woods, fiercely whipping the grass and trees. I had struggled just to climb up into my stand. At sunrise that morning, a wired-up, spooky doe had come by my stand, sending out an alert snort that lit up the swamp and shook me to my core. Few things are worse than getting caught on the hunt, and that doe had busted me big time.

But in spite of the bad weather and my bad luck, I stuck it out. I just couldn't give up the hunt for that day. Hours passed, and as I clung to that swaying tree, I could feel the frustration and defeat building in my brain. By late afternoon, I cracked; I knew that I'd waited until the deer would be up and moving around after their midday rest, but I'd had enough and decided to bail. I hadn't been back on solid ground for more than thirty seconds when, out of the corner of my eye, I saw Old Grey approaching, walking down the very trail I'd expected him to take—a trail I'd positioned my stand perfectly to overlook. In just seconds, he winded me, snorted, and was off and running. I still remember the boiling shame I felt, standing in that cold, windy woods, realizing that Old Grey wouldn't be back. That big-brained buck was gone for the season, because I hadn't used my *own* brain in making the call to either bail before it got too late or stick to my plan and wait for the hunt to unfold.

Odds are you've been caught in a similar bind. You're in a boardroom or giving a pitch, and you can feel the stakes rising. You've proposed a fee, but you're getting big push-back from your customer. If you lower your current proposal, you might open up a whole new bidding war. But if you don't, someone else might come in and take the business away. Do you stick it out or pivot?

There's a difference between overcoming adversity by pushing through tough days and riding out a losing battle without changing strategies. But it's rarely easy to know the difference. The ability to wait it out, to give your plan a chance to work, or to be still as you pull together a better strategy is the secret behind so many successful hunters. And as always, activity doesn't *guarantee* progress or results. My uncle, Michael Towbes, an incredibly successful banker, real estate investor, and philanthropist, summed up his career success in one simple statement: "I have never been afraid to miss a great deal." Those are profound words, worthy of following. But it takes real patience and practice to get good at knowing when to pivot and when to sit it out.

There isn't any hard-and-fast formula for making the call to stay or bail. The outcome of that decision will be determined by the experience, knowledge, intuition, and courage you bring to that particular event. But every time you find yourself at one of those "stick or bail" crossroads, you can rely on two guiding truths:

- **Earlier is better than later.** The longer you stick with a losing strategy, the less benefit you'll gain from an eventual pivot.
- **Know the cleanest way out before making your move.** Leaving a mess creates huge future distractions, hurdles, and other unnecessary challenges. Finding a thoughtful, clean exit can help you avoid the sometimes painful and expensive work of rebuilding a badly broken connection.

In business, we always have to make decisions about how far we're going to ride through a deal. There are times when it's best to cut your losses quickly. At other times it makes sense to push all the way through, even when the odds are stacked against you.

Business deals, processes, strategies, and relationships follow the same pattern. The longer you stay the course, the more you allow conditions, relationships, and expectations to form along one path—and the harder it's going to be for you to switch to a new path without causing major upheavals. If you pivot early, you aren't ditching a mature initiative; people are more flexible, more willing to consider new developments or ideas. But that flexibility fades over time. Think of late-stage changeups as akin to pulling a weed; the longer you let the roots develop, the harder the job becomes.

This leads us to the second guide for sitting it out: if you do decide to jump, make sure you have an exit strategy that leaves minimal destruction in its wake. That piece of advice may seem to contradict the previous one, but it doesn't. Let's say, for example, you've put somebody in charge of a team, and after giving him plenty of time (maybe too much time) to get his legs under them, you realize that he's simply not cut out for the job. You know you can't just walk into his office and tell him he's out, then call an immediate team meeting and announce that you've given their ex-leader the boot. If you do that, any plans or even minimal progress the group has been making will stop short.

Instead, you have to come up with a plan for systematically shifting the team's leadership: working more closely with the current leader to see whether you can help him up his game, bringing other team members into the decision-making process, finding a new assignment for the underperforming leader, and announcing the move well in advance to allow for a more fluid transition. You may not be able to jump immediately, but you can begin working your way out. Whatever your plan involves, you can't make the final exit until you've found a clean path out. Otherwise, you run the risk of compounding any trouble your pivot kicks up.

Closing with Command

I'm perched high up in a big aspen alongside a small lake in Antrim County, Michigan, with my bow drawn on a beautiful nine-point who's standing below me, thrashing his antlers against a nearby tree. He looks up the base of the tree I'm sitting in, and his eyes come all the way up to meet mine. But like all deer, this guy has really bad vision. He may *sense* that something's there, without really knowing that it's a predator. The shot angle is poor, and a solid hit doesn't seem likely, but I don't want any movement to give my position away. So I stand there, bow drawn. My heart is exploding in my chest, and the muscles in my back and shoulders are blazing in a blowtorch-hot burn. If there ever was an uncomfortable moment of silence, this is it; but I need to hold my position.

How many times have you been caught in that kind of face-off? You're in a meeting or in a confrontation with a partner, and at the most critical moment in the exchange, a silent stare-down ensues. The other person is locked on you, looking for any sign of movement, weakness, or uncertainty. You know that you can win if you can maintain silence, hold your position, and not crack—but can you do it? Not everyone can. In fact, right when they need to hang tough for just a bit longer is the point when most people get nervous. They start talking too soon and lose the opportunity to control the outcome.

I've experienced this moment countless times throughout my career, in my personal relationships, and in a tree stand: the time when I'm staring my win in the face, knowing that the trophy I've been pursuing is now mine, and I just have to claim it. Michael Waddell calls this moment "closing the coffin," and as blunt as that term is, it says it all for me. It's accurate, whether the end of my hunt involves taking an animal, signing the papers on a new home, or wrapping up a business deal. Why am I so fond of such a brutal statement? Because, like my friend Michael, I understand that when you're hunting, your Desired Outcome is to take the thing you've been hunting for. But to bring any hunt to a successful close, you have to be as strong at the finish as you are the first day you hit the trail. You have to close with command.

And, believe me, even experienced hunters have to practice and prepare for that final act. I've seen hardcore deer hunters fall victim to *buck fever*, a name we give to a condition in which you shake like a leaf when you finally draw down on your prey. And I've also seen many, *many* business people steer a deal through incredibly tough negotiations, only to go weak and lose focus when they hit the final stretch. Real-time execution demands that you bring it all home. That's why *closing with command* is an important part of any True Hunter's skill set.

When I worked in real estate, I knew a talented kid who had the potential to be great. He moved through deals with real skill—but the second he hit that 95 percent mark, he'd crumble. We'd be just about to close a major deal, and he would do something to sabotage it—not an intentional or even a conscious act, but something that broke our hold on the trophy. He'd knock off smaller deals every time. But when those "twelve-pointers" came around, he couldn't handle the idea of landing something really big.

I've blown the last moments of a deal myself, at times. My nerves get frayed, and I begin babbling, and even as I do it, I know it's a mistake—I know I'm turning myself from predator into prey, instead of holding my position, staying in command of my senses, and releasing my arrow at just the right time.

Those who can hold their command of the hunt through that uncomfortable moment of silence can close the coffin on whatever they're tracking. Your ability to be comfortable with the uncomfortable will help you maintain a kind of Zen-like control when it comes time to finalize the win in your hunt. When you learn to love the tension of closing, you'll have hit a breakthrough moment in your development as a True Hunter. Then you're on the way to more achievement in your life.

Even the most experienced hunters have to practice and prepare for the end of the hunt. It's like a muscle; when you stop working it, your strength fades. I keep my closing skills in shape with an exercise that involves two elements:

1. Knowing exactly what the target, the win, the Desired Outcome looks like
2. Constructing and rehearsing a mental image of the final moments of achieving your DO—imagining exactly what it will look like, feel like, smell like

The how-to of that first step should be familiar territory by now. Real-time execution allows you to adjust your goals as your hunt progresses, the data changes, targets fall out of reach, or new opportunities arise. So when you're heading into the final stages of any big pursuit, take time to revisit the outcome you're getting ready to lock up. Get a very clear picture of that DO in your mind. Think about why you want it, what kind of change it's going to represent.

Visualization is critical in this phase. As I draw down on a whitetail, for example, I'm in the consciousness zone, seeing a big-picture view of every step I've taken to reach this point—the ways the animal outsmarted me during the chase, the lessons this hunt has taught me about nature and survival and life, the ways I've grown as a hunter. I don't think, "I hope I don't blow this shot." Instead, my thoughts are more along the lines of "This is what I've been working toward. In this contest, I've won. The lessons I've learned in this hunt will shape all of my future hunts in some way. Now, I'm going to take this win cleanly, to claim this animal in a way that honors both of us and the process we've just been through."

Your thoughts shouldn't be much different when you're preparing to close a business deal. Instead of worrying "Will it work? Won't it? What do I do if the person across the table comes up with last-minute demands that I can't meet?" focus on your success at *wrapping up the deal*. Remind yourself of the goal you set out to achieve, and how you've made that DO yours. Think about what benefits the deal will bring to your business, about how pumped your team will be, what other doors this deal can open up for all of you. If you're closing the coffin on a professional relationship, remember exactly why you need to end the alliance, what benefits this closure will bring to your business or the rest of your team, and what it's going to mean—both good and bad—for the other party.

Whatever the DO, build a crystal-clear picture of the move you're about to take, so that when you walk into the boardroom or office where the final moments will go down, you know *exactly* what you're going in there to do—and what you're going to walk out with. That way, you can stay fluid if last-minute negotiations get heated, and you can respond to new data without losing focus on the DO you're shooting for. You may decide to settle for just part of the whole package, but you will know in advance precisely how much you're willing to negotiate away.

With the DO burned into your "mental retina," you're ready for the second part of your prep work. Create a clear picture in your mind of every person, event, and element of those final moments. To help with this process, I use my shoelace—the visualization tool I talked about back in Chapter One. If you've developed a similar tool or place or practice to help spark your meditation and visualization, this is the perfect time to use it. Close your eyes and imagine what the final moments of this hunt will look like, feel like, smell like, *be* like.

When I'm hunting whitetails and really in my zone, I know when I'm moving in on the final moment of the hunt. The action in the woods is on fire, the rut is in full swing, and I've located an area that's torn up, ripped apart, and stinking of deer. These are the breakthrough moments I live for. I begin checking the weather report last thing before I go to bed, so I can see which way the wind will be blowing at different times during the day. Then I begin to mentally walk through the coming day's hunt, beginning with the early hour when I'll be going in and the way the woods will feel and sound and smell before sunup. I have to start my visualization right at that point, because even though releasing the arrow will be the final event of the hunt, it's visualizing the entire process leading up to that moment that ups the odds of success.

I think about which stand I'll sit in and what angle I'll have to take if the leaves are off the trees, so I have an adequate backdrop behind me. Then I see myself in the stand, as the animal makes his way toward me. I see the animal move into perfect range; I imagine at what point I'll make my move, draw my bow, release the arrow. In essence, I've experienced all these critical moments of the hunt well before I actually walk into the woods.

You can benefit from the same kind of detailed visualization. Before the closing of any negotiation or business deal, ask yourself:

1. What are you going to feel like as you enter the room?
2. What will the room look like? What sounds will you hear around you?
3. What seat at the table are you going to take when you walk in there? If that seat's taken, what's your next choice? Where do you think each person on your team should be sitting in relationship to you?
4. Who's going to open in the meeting? How are you going to open? How are you going to lay out your desired outcomes?
5. Who's going to be the closer? Who's going to say, "This has been a great meeting—now what are the next steps?"

Small details, like the way you're positioned around the negotiating table, can make a huge psychological difference for everyone involved in the deal. I prefer to have the opener sit to the left side of the table and the closer to the right, so the closer is positioned like the period at the end of a sentence. I build a visualization of the closing moments that takes in all this information and more. I imagine sitting down in the office or at the conference room table, drinking from a bottle of water, hearing the buzz of business going on outside the room, saying what I have to say, listening to the response, and shaking the hand of the person I'm doing business with. I go over the scenario multiple times, each time tweaking this moment or that, so that I've imagined my responses to a number of variables. This level of detail may seem obsessive, but it provides a True Hunter with the clarity and focus necessary to take a trophy.

Not everyone's strong in every moment of closing a deal. Carefully choose the roles each member of your team will play, so that you're leveraging everyone's talents. Then talk through the closing together. You want your team to be as practiced in those final moments as you are, so that all of you will execute fluidly and flawlessly when your performance matters most. By embedding your vision of the final moments of the deal firmly in your consciousness, you create a template that you can rely on to guide you, even when totally unexpected events unfold. You'll walk into the closing knowing exactly what you're there to do.

Success is all about the journey—the excitement of the chase, the thrill of knowing you're prepped for action and poised to win, the pure joy of being really challenged and tested in your element. But ultimately all great hunters have to be well practiced in doing what they set out to do. In business, it can be easy to lose your focus as you near the final moments of your project or pursuit. Or you can become queasy when it's time to end a business relationship or cut away dying portions of the organization. That's why it's so important to train yourself to take those kinds of final, decisive actions: moving your prey into range, closing in on your target, and keeping your guard up as you draw closer to nailing your deal, negotiation, or other endpoint.

So use the two-part visualization described earlier to develop a True Hunter's skill at wrapping up the hunt. You'll be amazed at how much stronger and more effective your performance becomes when you learn to create and rehearse strong visualizations. Your plans will be better, and you will be focused and prepared when it comes time to release the arrow on your target.

Write It Out

Just writing down what you want to achieve improves your chances of achieving it. Follow this simple process for getting your DO clear in your mind and improving your chances of nailing it:

1. When you clearly understand your DO, write it down on paper.

2. Look at that written goal multiple times in the days before you move in to close the deal.

3. With that paper in hand, test the outcome in your mind by visualizing what the win will look and feel like.

4. Read the written DO before you walk into your final meeting or negotiation, then put the paper somewhere in your notes or in your pocket, and take it with you.

You may have trouble getting into this process at first, but it's well worth your time to practice it. Remember, the best form of real-time execution is the one that gets you to the win. This exercise can speed you on your way.

Breaking Through, Breaking Out

The better you become at building the pillars of The Hunt into your daily life—seeing with consciousness, acting with authenticity, leveraging every opportunity— the better you'll be at achieving the thrilling ride of real-time execution. But you don't want to lose yourself in the momentum of progress. A full life doesn't happen on autopilot, and you can't sustain real-time execution if you don't mark the significant milestones along the path toward your DOs. Those important markers can be made up of just about any kind of moment you can imagine— landing a job, getting a first date with someone you've been dying to spend time with, or finding the home you've been hunting for. But whatever their specific details, most milestones fall into one of two categories:

- **Breakthrough Moments:** A breakthrough happens when you crack the code, finally land on the solution, learn the technique, find the missing piece, correct the misalignment, or otherwise grab hold of the key to the locked door that's been blocking your progress.
- **Breakout Moments:** Breakout moments are those times when you get the trophy you've been chasing—the job, the mate, the peace of mind—the prize your breakthrough moment allowed you to close in on. They come to you when your model has paid off—and they become common once you achieve the state of flow, which we talk about in the closing chapter of this book.

We create breakout moments through the care and feeding of breakthrough moments along the way. Both are woven into the fabric of real-time execution, and recognizing and celebrating all of them is essential to your progress as a True Hunter. These achievements help you learn, grow, and become both more skillful at taking the trophies you're gunning for and more proud and grateful for the experience. By learning to honor the breakthrough and breakout moments in your hunt, you'll be feeding better performance and more successful outcomes down the road—and that's real-time execution at its finest.

Josh Linkner—CEO and managing partner of Detroit Venture Partners, five-time tech entrepreneur, and *New York Times* best-selling author—knows all about the value of honoring small moments of success. In his book *Disciplined Dreaming*, Linkner writes about the power of breakthrough creativity to fuel fast-paced, innovative execution in any organization.[2] To promote a culture of innovation in any environment, he recommends that we not only celebrate the small wins from creative ideas, but also reward efforts that don't necessarily hit the bull's-eye. In fact, Linkner says that he considers many of the small setbacks that others might call "failures" to be *experiments*. Truly great trophies are rarely easy to take. We know by now that The Hunt isn't an event; it's a process, a *series of steps* that include some stumbles and some breakthrough moments that, together, keep moving you forward toward your targeted outcome.

If you don't observe and embrace the small wins on your way to your hunt's final moments, you can lose your focus on the big issues that made the pursuit worthwhile in the first place. It's critical, when taking any trophy, to congratulate yourself, your team, and your family for grabbing the prizes you've all earned. And it's perfectly okay to want some accolades. If you don't keep some kind of score, you lose some of the power behind your will to win. So feel free to love the breakout moments—expect them, thrive in them, feel good that you've earned them. Just don't forget to celebrate the breakthrough moments that get you there. Remember, *all* of these wins contribute to the state of real-time execution that will continue to move you forward toward your ultimate goals—and through a life full of satisfaction and achievement.

The Last Thirty Minutes of Daylight

Here are the critical ideas to carry with you as you leave this chapter—ideas that will help make real-time execution part of your primal nature as you move through any hunt.

- **Expect change.** Pursue your DOs carefully, and then track both macro and micro data to stay locked in on your target's trail.
- **See the data clearly, so you're ready to pivot.** You know it's time to pivot when your tracking and targeting data reveals a serious vulnerability in your model—one representing leverage that your competitors can use to make *you* their prey.
- **Know your model.** You never know where your next competitor will come from. When you know your own model inside and out, you're positioned to build barriers to prevent competitors from entering your space—from any direction.
- **Make radical shifts through a series of smaller pivots.** Stay just far enough ahead of trends to own

them, without going so far ahead of the pack that you become a target.

- **Don't make the move into new territory just to be a "me too."** Go in prepared to be the lion, ready to own the new space.

- **Sometimes the best move is *no move* at all.** If you're going to sit out bad weather, dig in and continue to follow your plan. If you're going to split, do it early enough that you can leave without destroying any chance for a successful hunt when the weather clears.

- **Practice closing the coffin.** Revisit your DOs and form a crystal-clear image of exactly what success looks like for this hunt. Then visualize every moment of the closing process and rehearse it—and its multiple variations—until you have the entire scene embedded in your memory.

- **Be there for the breakthroughs.** Be conscious, present, and aware in the hunt, so you can honor and celebrate the breakthrough moments that make the breakout moment of success possible.

FINDING FLOW AND
LEAVING A CLEAN WAKE

Hunter, husband, CEO—I wear a lot of titles. But I never forget that what I *truly* am is a human being, a role I succeed in by being at home in my skin and at peace with the world I live in. A big-picture perspective matters to me, not just because it helps me understand the challenges and opportunities around me. It also keeps me very aware of my tiny role in a very big, complicated, and connected world. I know that nothing happens in isolation in this life. Before I act, I make it a point to think about how my actions will play out. I try to imagine how they'll shape my hunt, the world around me, and the experience of all of us who live in it. I'm in the hunt to win, but I don't believe in winning at any cost. In fact, I'm a spiritual person—just like most of the True Hunters I know.

Don't let the term "spiritual" spook you. Being a successful hunter involves a certain level of faith in the power of the natural order and your ability to succeed within it. You never hear True Hunters talk about "conquering" nature. Whether it's building a business, outperforming a competitor, creating a secure and satisfying life for their family, strengthening their community, or taking a trophy buck, True Hunters achieve their goals by learning to be a powerful force *within* the natural order. We use our human capabilities to leverage the nonstop opportunities life sends our way, and the power of that momentum keeps us moving on to the next hunt, the next achievement, and the next breakthrough moment. When you bring the pillars of The Hunt to your pursuits, you position yourself for just that kind of lifelong achievement. You have faith in your vision, your methods, your decisions, your skills, and your motivations, and faith in the natural order. You aren't just hunting in your life; you are *living* The Hunt. And you're finding the flow that carries all True Hunters forward.[1]

Flow is a term for the kind of intense, focused, self-propelled, outcome-oriented experiences you've been learning about through this book. Finding flow is the primary work of The Hunt—work that is its own reward. Our ability to successfully leverage the skills we build over our lifetime and to continue honing those skills is the true trophy we take from life. When you understand that, every day's hunt falls into place as another step along your path. You can expect that path to bring more hunts, more allies, more learning experiences, more wins, more *life* your way. Finding flow is the ultimate payoff you get from bringing the pillars of The Hunt into your own approach to life. And that's an outcome that benefits everyone—the hunter, the hunted, and the world we all walk through.

Getting in Flow

The word "flow" has been around for a long time; in fact, some researchers think it's one of the oldest words used on the planet.[2] The ancient roots of the word make perfect sense, because it describes an almost primal process in which any number of individual elements—drops of water, grains of sand, migrating birds, whatever—come together and then move in a fluid but connected "whole" in a single direction. And like the flowing water that carved out the Grand Canyon, the power of flow can be mighty. That's the experience of The Hunt: by aligning your actions and decisions with your authentic motivations and skill sets, ultimate goals, and true Desired Outcomes, you put yourself in the most powerful position possible for achieving results. That's how you *live* The Hunt. You're aware of your individual actions, but powered through them by the real-time, evolving effect of their combined momentum.

When you're hunting in flow, you accomplish one step, then the next and the next and the next, and soon you find yourself moving toward the finish line, pumped and ready for the next ride. All of those positive results generate an abundance of positive energy. This process allows you not only to achieve the DOs you've set out to take down on this hunt, but also to actually pull *more* potential success into your path. You meet more of the people you need to know, uncover more creative ideas, take bolder steps, find bigger wins, and leave a wake of success and possibility that makes everything and everyone around you better. Flow may sound incredible—because it is. But it's also very real.

As much as the process sounds like a bolt from the blue, it doesn't just happen by accident or to a chosen few. Flow naturally follows real-time execution, which—as you've seen—is the result of

- Climbing up above your ego, where you can view yourself and the world around you with consciousness and clarity, aware and alive and present in every step of your hunt
- Living in the *real* world with authenticity, knowing who you are and what you want out of life, and dealing with people and events as they *really are*—not as you wish they were or fear they may be
- Learning to spot and capitalize on *every* event and opportunity, using leverage to power your progress toward your target—and to bring new targets into your focus

When you're hunting in the field, you just *know* the buck is coming your way, but that knowing isn't some psychic phenomenon; it's your interpretation of data. You've studied and leveraged the variables. You've studied your animal, positioned yourself in the right spot, and planned your movements in synch with the season, the weather, and the prevailing conditions of the territory. You've *seen* the successful outcome playing out in your mind. When this bump or that pothole has appeared in your path, you've been ready and able to skirt it and keep moving forward. Because you've *known* where you're headed, obstacles are momentary interruptions or detours in your progress, not dead ends that stop you cold. You can have faith that everything is going to come together just the way you've planned for it. So when that trophy moves into your shooting range, you're ready to close this hunt with focus and purpose, and then move on to the next. That's flow.

I try to stay in flow as much as possible in my life. I *expect* success, because I've covered the ground necessary to reach it.

I once went on a trip to Cuba with a group of business leaders. I left for this trip expecting to gain some wins from it—speaking opportunities, powerful connections, and a new understanding of a nation, economic setup, and culture with which I had no previous experience. All of that happened, just as I thought it would.

Now, I could have spent my time in Cuba missing my family back home, worrying about how things were going at the office, or focused on some kind of hypercritical judgment of communism. A trip bounded by that kind of negativity would have been the ultimate waste of time and energy, an experience that—at best—would knock me sideways instead of moving me forward. Instead, I generated new third-party connections with people and organizations I had never worked with before. I had key meetings with some people I had been trying to get in front of for months. And I learned that Cuba and its people are a whole lot more than just a "communist country." That trip flowed for me, because I made it happen. I did the things I knew I had to do to position myself so that these results would come to me, and then they did.

Aligning with Life

Flow is about living in rhythm with the world around you. You hit that rhythm by aligning your ideas and actions so that your momentum *pulls* you toward your DOs, instead of trying to *push* your way through to achieving them. When you're in flow, moving with the real-time events and data around you, you can almost hear the harmony of your progress playing in your head.

Flow helps you surf the waves of the world around you instead of fighting against the tide. That kind of coordinated progress moves you forward more quickly and easily than the struggle ever could. And because the natural world moves in flow, you're really just trying to tap into that bigger river of momentum. You can get stuck going 35 in a 50 mph stretch of roadway, and if you allow yourself to trust in the flow around you, to move in a stream with the other traffic, you'll usually start catching a green light now and then, find a workable detour, or simply adjust to the slower speed and—one way or another—arrive in time for whatever you're moving toward. Of course, you *could* try to buck the flow by slamming back and forth between lanes, riding the bumper of the car in front of you, or shouting obscenities at the jerks around you who are doing the same thing. Ever tried that? If so, I bet you know how useless it is.

That's the difference between finding flow and fighting the tide. You're in alignment with life, so hitting a traffic jam is just a natural part of your journey for the day. Either it's a normal rush-hour experience, which you bought into by driving in this place during this time, or there's something out of the ordinary going on up ahead, which presents you with a situation you can either accept or abandon at the first exit ramp. You can find a way to use the time spent in traffic—listening to music or books, thinking through issues you'll need to take care of when you hit your destination, or just practicing patience—but once you're in a traffic jam, it's yours to deal with.

In every area of your life, the world will sometimes throw obstacles at you that can put a serious kink in your flow. So what? Moving fluidly in, around, and through obstacles is what a skillful hunt is all about. But you're the only one who can stop your movement altogether. Anger and ego will knock you out of alignment and stall your progress every time.

But I hope that you've also seen how I've "eaten" all of the lessons dished up by my experiences—the incredible leg-up of self-confidence and business savvy I got from my parents; the predatory skills and understanding of nature I gained from a lifetime of hunting; the ego-checking lessons in personal growth dealt out to me during the WHA fiasco. Every step—and stumble—along that trail has made me a smarter man, a more responsible family member, and a stronger leader. And it's helped me learn to keep every subsequent step in alignment with the overall direction I've set for my life. Everyone's life, including mine, is a work in progress.

Of course, to get in alignment with your destiny, you need a really clear idea of what your ultimate life goals actually entail. Some Desired Outcomes are relatively easy to ID. Short-term goals—like landing a promotion, buying or selling a home, or learning a new language—are driven by circumstance and the moving flow of our lives. Opportunities arise; needs evolve; circumstances change. That's why our DOs need to be clear and well-defined, but also flexible enough to allow us to grow in our hunt.

But ultimate goals—*life* goals—are bigger than most Desired Outcomes. When you're deciding where you want your life to take you, you have to go deep. Whatever Q&A you have to undergo to choose a Desired Outcome takes on about one hundred times the importance and detail when you're considering the overall direction for your life. Those ultimate goals have to stand up to some of the toughest questions you'll ever have ask yourself—and they fall into three main categories:

1. **What meaning does this goal have?** You might say to yourself, "I want to make a million dollars by the time I'm thirty," but what will it mean if you do? Do you care *how* you make all that money? Would you still be happy if you made it by the time you were thirty-five? What if you made $900,000 by the time you were thirty; would that be nothing but a disappointment to you?

Or let's say your goal is to get married and raise children. Again, what is it about that goal that matters most to you? What part of having those kids do you most want to experience? What does having a family *really mean* to you? Would you be unwilling to marry someone who didn't want kids, but who you were wild about? Would you marry someone you *weren't* that in love with, rather than be single?

Maybe you want to devote yourself to conservation. What does that mean to you—protecting the environment from the destructive impact of people? Or making the natural world more accessible to more people? Are you ready to direct your life toward this effort, through hands-on field work or organizing or political lobbying? Or are you really just interested in being a good citizen of the earth?

You get the picture. You have to dig down into the real reasons you've decided that this choice is a meaningful direction for your life and then fully understand what that meaning is.

2. **What purpose does this goal have?** This question—along with all those that go into answering it—is similar to finding your goal's meaning. However, it requires that you ask more about the outcomes:

- What will you *do* with those million bucks? Will you stop pushing to earn more at that point—or will you then set a new income target?
- How will marriage change your life? What will you be able to do, enjoy, or experience that you can't as a single person? What about those kids? What do you expect them to do for your life?
- What DOs can you envision for your work in conservation? How will it improve your community, region, state, country, or the world?

3. **Is it big enough?** Now we're hitting the nitty-gritty: are the ultimate goals you've chosen *worth* investing your life in? And are they important enough to keep you on the trail through the years ahead? When you've answered

all of the category 1 and 2 questions in this list, you should have the information you need to answer this category 3 monster. No *single* goal is likely to do it for you. Yes, you want a family; but you also want work you enjoy and a life that feeds your soul, grows your mind, and expands your connection to the world around you. Imagine yourself ten years down the road, then another ten, and so on. Are you still happy and fulfilled on this hunt? What if you died tomorrow? Would you feel that you'd died in pursuit of the things that matter most to you?

Every pillar of The Hunt you've learned about in this book helps keep your choices and actions in alignment with your ultimate goals, because

- **You've replaced confusion with consciousness**, by awakening your primal instincts and expanding your awareness. You aren't sleepwalking through life, stumbling in the dark, mindlessly following the herd or chasing after shadows. You're alive to the world and to the way you're moving through it.
- **You've replaced ego with authenticity.** Instead of struggling to maintain an image, you're expressing your authentic nature in just about every aspect of your life. You know who you are and where you're headed. You're open to possibility, but you aren't leaving your outcomes to luck. You're the able navigator.

- **You know how to use the tools you have and find the opportunities life sends your way.** You're a super-predator whose choices aren't guided by limitation. Rather, you're surrounded by an endless stream of options for leverage, and you have the confidence and skill sets you need to maximize them all.

- **You aren't invested in digging in and defending your life against change.** As a True Hunter, your life is about movement and pursuit. You remain focused on the next challenge, the next hunt, and you're pumped up about moving on. That means your choices naturally link up, joining forces and building momentum as they carry you on toward the ultimate goals that make up the hunt of your life.

Big issues require big understanding and offer big rewards, and finding flow is one of the biggest rewards you can bring to your life. By learning about and understanding the pillars of The Hunt, you've prepared to think about your life through a panoramic lens that allows you to see how you're connected to the rest of the world, and how each of your decisions guides your life journey. You're ready to address the big picture questions that will align your thoughts and actions and ideas with the most important decision you can make—what do you want to do with your life? You may not know the answer today. But don't worry; you don't have to. You just have to start *asking the questions*, actively thinking about meaning and purpose, and letting those thoughts guide your day-to-day choices about how you'll spend your time, energy, and focus. Just by wading into those waters, you're entering the flow of life.

You also don't have to worry about *forcing* your life into alignment. Throughout this book we've talked about ideas and practices that naturally move your choices, your actions, your understanding in alignment with your life. The trickier issue is learning to *stay* in alignment. When it comes to carving your path through life, the most dangerous detours can seem like the most attractive options. That's where your ultimate life goals become your safeguards. Think of them as something like those fluorescent metal lane markers and rumble strips that keep you in your driving lane.

Whenever you reach a branch in your path, test all potential options against your ultimate goals. If an immediate choice doesn't fit with the long-range goals you're tracking down, then you know it's a no-go. Very few of us actually "jump the lane"; that is, make a single decision or take a particular action that causes them to go completely off course. Instead, we tend to wander; we move just outside the boundaries of our values, principles, and goals, then drift a little bit further off course, then further, and before you know it, we've been off the trail for so long we can't even see our way back or remember what we were heading toward. But if you make it a practice to test your decisions against your ultimate goals, you'll have the rumble strips in place to warn you when you first begin to drift off course. Then you can decide what needs to change; your short-term direction or your long-range target.

I've had to make those same kinds of drift tests at OHub, and they've resulted in a number of shifts. I saw the potential when we first pivoted from the WHA to our new business model. I made a commitment to one critical DO: to make this brand as big as it could possibly be. I realized that in order to do that, I had to take it through three levels. First, we needed a *viable business model.* Second, we had to become the *best business-to-business organization* in our arena. Third, we'd have to take our *model directly to consumers.*

I had known that I would be the right leader for the organization during the first two steps of the process. But I also knew that I would be moving out of my authentic territory when we started the climb into the third level. I would need to stay focused on my hunt and turn the leadership of OHub over to someone whose skills were better aligned with its new direction—a leader who could take it through that section of the trail.

After some heavy scouting and a long search, I landed the right leader—someone I knew would be able to take OHub to the next level. That decision freed me up to keep moving down the path toward the ultimate goals I've set for myself. I felt comfortable because I knew I'd made sure that OHub had the leadership it needed. At the same time, I positioned myself to bring my professional life more closely in alignment with the DOs and ultimate goals I'd been chasing.

Within just a few months, everyone was able to relax and see the benefits of all that realignment. Now the business is moving forward with real-time execution. That doesn't mean that the shift took place without a hitch. We had arguments, we hit potholes, we had to tweak processes and practices. But in the end everyone—even the folks who told me I was crazy to make the move—agrees that OHub has never been tighter, more efficient, better positioned to own its territory. In other words, the company is in alignment with the destiny we *all* envisioned for it.

Think of alignment as *power*—to move forward, build momentum, and achieve. As you carve the path toward the outcomes and goals you've chosen in your personal and professional life, keep checking your progress for drift. Be present, be aware, and most important, *be real*. We get only one life. If we spend too much of it hunting down the wrong trails, we run the real risk of running out of time and energy before we even get close to our target.

Leaving a Clean Wake

Seasons change. As a hunter, I don't lead a climate-controlled life, and I don't track seasonal shifts by watching the changing promotional displays at the drugstore. But, as much as my awareness is tied to the seasons, I don't get too emotional about the passage of time. That's part of the True Hunter thing, too. Life isn't a series of straight lines that begin at Point A and end at Point B. Life is a cycle, and hunters get that completely. A season isn't a season if it never ends; a living thing isn't a living thing if it doesn't die. It's not that we're not moved by death. We know what death looks like, and we also know that every year, we're getting closer to our own.

But one of the biggest lessons we all can learn from nature is that every death is a beginning. A tree falls, and hundreds—thousands—of other life forms surge forward, fed, sheltered, or given a new opportunity to thrive by this stage in the tree's cycle. And life is all cycles, curving pathways, winding rivers, crashing waves—flow.

When you're hunting in flow, you know that where you are now isn't where you'll always be. The season will change. This hunt will end, and another will begin. The river bends, but the water keeps flowing. A True Hunter isn't concerned about stopping that forward movement. Rather, he cares about *feeding* it, building momentum and leveraging past successes—not resting on them. And, maybe of greatest importance, every True Hunter is concerned about leaving a *clean wake*—a clear, healthy trail that offers as much opportunity to the hunters who follow as it offered to those who went before.

The idea of leaving the path a better place than it was when you found it isn't particularly difficult to grasp.

It *can* be totally confusing, though, to listen to the people who *don't* get it. I once heard some people discussing how a new bill that was making its way through Congress would shape the environment one hundred years down the road. One of these guys said, "Well, I'm not going to be around in a hundred years, so the people who are alive then will have to figure it out." Now, I'd bet that just about everyone reading this book would call that statement shockingly stupid. But a lot of people live their lives with the same total disregard for the future that those words demonstrate. Instead of leaving a clean wake for the folks who follow, these people just keep walking away from all of the messes that they've either created, contributed to, or done nothing to prevent. And, whether they know it or not, the mess is going to come back and bite them. That's not some kind of magical karma; it's reality. It's how *a cycle* works. So, leaving a clean wake is not just a good idea. It's a form of self-preservation—for you, your family, your business, your planet.

Leaving a clean wake means much more than being a good steward of nature, although that's one of the most important responsibilities we have. It's just as important to be a good steward of the personal and professional world you build and live in. That's what leaving a clean wake means: approaching the need to follow a new direction honestly; tying up loose ends, swallowing your ego, and supporting new ideas, structures, and visions. It requires that you build an environment—a *culture*—that's strong enough to shape the DNA of everyone in it in a way that promotes new life and drives success. You're leaving behind a place that you would be happy to find yourself walking into again, if the cycle of your life brought you there. You know this stuff; you just have to remember to live it.

Now, I'm going to branch off from this hunt and leave you to follow your own path forward for a while. That's not to say that I'm tagging out, or that our trails won't cross again. We're hunting the same territory, after all; we all want to leverage our human nature for all it's worth, to push our primal instincts to the next level, to get our energy and interests in alignment with the great flow of life around us. This book is just the beginning of my journey down a new trail, and I look forward to many more opportunities to share that hunt with you. In the meantime, I've left you with a lot of useful tools, ideas, and techniques you can use to make your hunt more meaningful and productive. Grab your gear and hit the woods, hunter. And never forget that success is always in season—and The Hunt is on.

NOTES

Chapter 1

1. Colorado Parks and Wildlife includes this kind of visualization among its ten tips for elk hunters: http://wildlife.state .co.us/HUNTING/ELKHUNTINGUNIVERSITY/3/Pages /TipsforHuntingColoradoElk.aspx.

2. You can find Ford's specific quote, along with others, in "21 Quotes from Henry Ford on Business, Leadership and Life," Erica Anderson, *Forbes.com*, May 31, 2013.

3. Scott Feinberg, "Telluride: Robert Redford Feted with Career Tribute," August 2013; http://www.hollywoodreporter.com /race/telluride-robert-redford-feted-career-618016.

4. Julie Huffaker, "Leadership Development: Listening Like Robert Redford (And How It Makes You Taller)," http://www .hungrytoolkit.com/leadership-development-listening-like -robert-redford-and-how-it-makes-you-taller/.

Chapter 2

1. James Wallace and Jim Erickson, *Hard Drive: Bill Gates and the Making of the Microsoft Empire* (New York: Wiley, 1992).

2. *Steve Jobs*, Walter Isaacson (New York: Simon & Schuster, 2011).

3. Kathleen Davis, "Inside Richard Branson's Unconventional Business Approach," *Entrepreneur.com*, October 12, 2012. http://www.entrepreneur.com/blog/224599.

4. Richard Branson, "Richard Branson on When Inexperience Is an Advantage," Inspiration Station, *Entrepreneur.com*, November 2011. http://www.entrepreneur.com/article/220789.

5. Richard Branson, *Business Stripped Bare: Adventures of a Global Entrepreneur* (London: Virgin Books, 2010).

6. You can find Richard Branson's blog, links to all of his books, and more information about the Virgin Group at http://www.virgin.com/richard-branson.

7. There's a lot of controversy around whether Ruth truly was calling his shot. Father Gabe Costa wrote a series of in-depth articles based on sports historian William Jenkinson's analysis of that event. You can find the series at http://newyork.cbslocal.com/2012/09/04/by-the-numbers-babe-ruths-called-shot-eight-decades-later-part-1/.

8. You can learn more about Susan Scott, her organization, and her publications and workshops at http://www.fierceinc.com/index.php. Scott's book *Fierce Conversations: Achieving Success at Work & in Life, One Conversation at a Time*, was published by Penguin Group/Viking Studio in 2002.

Chapter 3

1. Check out the PAW calculator on my website, davidfarbman.com, to help determine the time of day when you're hitting your own peak performance.

2. "Clover Technologies Group Once Again Ranks in the Top 100 Fastest-Growing Private Companies in America for the Third Year in a Row," Clover Technologies, *PRNewswire*, November 1, 2004. www.prnewswire.com.

Chapter 4

1. Clare O'Connor, "The Mystery Monk Making Billions with 5-Hour Energy," *Forbes.com*, February 8, 2012. http://www .forbes.com/sites/clareoconnor/2012/02/08/manoj-bhargava -the-mystery-monk-making-billions-with-5-hour-energy/2/.
2. Josh Linkner, *Disciplined Dreaming: A Proven System to Drive Breakthrough Creativity* (San Francisco: Jossey-Bass, 2011).

Chapter 5

1. Dr. Mihaly Csikszentmihalyi was one of the first people to write about the state of flow. I recommend his book *Flow: The Psychology of Optimal Experience* (New York: HarperCollins, 1990). His 2004 TED talk, "Flow: The Secret to Happiness," is available at http://www.ted.com/talks/mihaly_csikszent mihalyi_on_flow.html.
2. Mark Pagela, Quentin D. Atkinsonc, Andreea S. Caluded, and Andrew Meadea, "Ultraconserved Words Point to Deep Language Ancestry Across Eurasia," *Proceedings of the National Academy of Science of the United States of America* (*PNAS*) 110(21), May 21, 2013.

ACKNOWLEDGMENTS

A lot of people have helped shape the ideas and experiences that led me to write *The Hunt*, but my family has been the beating heart of that process. I want to thank my mom and dad for introducing me to hunting and for encouraging me to be passionate and follow my dreams. I also thank my brother Andy, who, in addition to being an incredible partner in business, has taught me that blood really *is* thicker than water. Panda, without your support I would never have created OutdoorHub, nor would I have written this book. And I especially want to thank my wife, Nadine, and my three boys, Hunter, River, and Fischer, who make every sunrise and sunset more special. I feel so blessed to have such an amazing family that supports my obsession with the outdoors and passionate commitment to living life to the fullest.

Friends and fellow hunters have walked this trail with me, too. I'm sending out a big thank-you to Gary Strange, who taught me to deer hunt, and to Jay Livingston and Eric Cherry. You guys are my first and second phone calls for hunting updates, and I love you. I'm grateful to all of my awesome hunting pals, and to everyone who enjoys the great outdoors. It has taken me years to realize the importance of simply loving the hunt, but now I get it. This book is about just that. I also want to thank Pete Davis, my most trusted friend and ally when it comes to helping each other through good times or bad. A huge thank-you goes out to one of my best friends, Rob Goldman; I'd be lost without his advice, support, and love. You're the man, Rob! I also would like to thank Toni Ventimiglia, Heather Stewart, Ethan Chamberlin, and Guy Schueller for their belief in Carbon Media Group and in me, as a friend. To the great teams at Carbon Media Group, Farbman Group, and Nuco Health—thanks for being awesome. All of the guys in the Old School and Kompressor forums have helped me too, by pushing me to keep it real and be my best. And, of course, I'm also grateful to all of my investors who backed me when I went into business in the great outdoors.

A lot of heavy lifting goes into getting a book into print. I want to thank Lauren Kerwin, Eleni Kelakos, Alesya Opelt, and Amie Kuciban for their constant and much-needed help in managing the writing process. I owe a big round of thanks to Josh Linkner for his friendship as well as his excellent advice and encouragement. And I want to thank Lorna Gentry, who helped me pull this vision together, along with Karen Murphy, Christine Moore, and John Maas of Jossey-Bass, whose expert guidance helped turn that vision into a book we all can be proud of. Without their support, this book would be merely an unfulfilled dream. Above all, I want to thank my agent, Esmond Harmsworth, for his savvy leadership and keen insights, as well as for his hard work and support.

The Hunt wouldn't have been complete without the contributions of the many friends, hunters, and colleagues who took time to speak with me about their own hunt for success. Thanks for putting up with my requests for interviews and advice. Your wisdom has added so much to this book. Special thanks to Dan Gilbert, who, in even a quick conversation, can amp me up and transform my way of thinking. And I'm sending another special shout-out to my boys at *Michael Waddell's Bone Collector:* Michael Waddell, Nick Mundt, Travis "T-Bone" Turner, and Jim Schiefelbein. We are always there for each other, and I will always be your Yankee pal from Michigan.

Lastly, I am incredibly grateful to Ellsworth, Michigan, and its unreal beauty. So many of my connections to the outdoors—and the universe—have developed within the area north of the 45th parallel, and I cherish every moment I am able to spend there. A lifetime of hunting and hanging at Timber Ridge Ranch has made me the man I am today.

ABOUT THE AUTHOR

David Farbman is the founder and chairman of Carbon Media Group, the world's leading online media company dedicated to the outdoors, and a principal in NAI Farbman Group, a full-service real estate firm. Farbman serves as CEO of Nuco Health, a highly specialized revenue cycle management company dedicated to helping hospital systems increase overall revenue and profitability. A life-long hunter and outdoorsman, Farbman shares his passion for nature, leadership, and solutions-based organizational management through his website and blog and in speaking engagements.

Farbman was instrumental in sparking the Downtown Detroit residential market and is an owner of several high-rise office buildings along the Detroit skyline. A member of the executive board of Young Presidents' Organization and the Center For Exceptional Families, he also has served on numerous boards, including those of the Detroit Economic Development Corporation, the Detroit Economic Growth Corporation, and the Detroit Regional Chamber. Farbman was a founding member and past chairman of Beyond Basics, a nonprofit organization devoted to improving literacy rates among public school children.

Farbman lives with his family in Bingham Farms, Michigan. For more information, please visit www .davidfarbman.com.

INDEX

A

Acceptance, 57

Achievement: lifelong, 184;
measurable, 29, 49

Action, taking: demand for,
78, 85; freedom from fear
through, 25; movement in,
41; readiness for, 74–75; that
maintains strong relationships, 84; training yourself
for, 176

Actions: aligning, 185;
responsibility for, 77; targeting all, 123

Adaptability, 4, 37, 42, 70, 120.
See also Flexibility

AgHub, 137

Agility/nimbleness, 148, 152

Alertness, 156

Alignment, 8, 185, 188–197,
200. *See also* Flow

Alliances: building, investing in,
51–52, 75–78, 80; dysfunctional, avoiding dealing with,
87–88; ending, 87–91, 172;
forming the Bone Collector
Brotherhood, 81–83; honest,
laying the groundwork for, 54;
leveraging, 133; maintaining,
investing in, 51–52, 83–87,
94; ongoing maintenance of,
118; strong, forming, 78–81;
value of, 75–76, 81

Allies: confidence in, 78; gaining
long-term, 5; lies weakening
relationships with, 71

Amazon, 147

American Revolution campaign,
162

Anger, 84, 90, 189–190

Anticipating next moves, 40,
115–116, 125–128, 142

211

Apple, 56

Authentic nature: acceptance of your, 57; being real about your, 52, 93; core element of our, as unchanging, 60–61; expressing your, 193; finding people who can deal with your, 78, 79–80; reminding yourself of your, 92; seeing someone else's, 118

Authenticity: addressing, exercises for, 57–58, 61; alignment resulting from, 193; aspects of, described, 51–93; benefits of, 52–53; and the Bone Collector, 58–62, 76, 81–83; brand, fighting to maintain, 161; Branson's form of, 62–63; Brink's unique brand of maintaining, 3, 161–163; and building alliances, 51–52, 75–78, 80; and claiming your native territory, 59–62; and ending alliances, 87–91; and forming strong alliances, 78–81; getting better at building, benefit of, 178; helping with finding leverage points, 131; importance of, 51–52; key ideas about, 93–94; and maintaining alliances, 51–52, 83–87; and marking your target, 63–70; in message

delivery, 70; overcoming negativity through, 91–93; overview of, 6–7; and owning your outcomes, 72–75, 94; path to, 4; personal brand of, establishing and expressing your, 56–58; resulting in real-time execution, 186; and shedding the camouflage, 51, 57–58, 91–93; and tracking peak activity periods, 108; and the truth about lies, 71

Avoidance, problem with, 87–88, 91

Awareness, 25, 48, 181, 193, 198. *See also* Being there; Consciousness

B

Backpedaling, 74

Being there, 22–25, 49, 156–158, 181

Bhargava, Manoj, 158–159

Big picture, seeing the, 16, 18, 24, 25, 37, 48, 49, 149, 171, 183, 194. *See also* Consciousness

Bitterness, 111

Blaming, 73, 74, 118

Blockbuster, 152

Bluffing, 53

Body language, attention to, 157

Bone Collector Brotherhood, 3, 58–59, 76, 81–83

Borders, 152

Boundaries, looking beyond, 160

Branson, Richard, 62–63, 202n6

Breakout moments, 152, 178, 179, 181

Breakthrough moments, 144, 163, 170, 173, 178, 179, 180, 181, 184

Brink, Kim, 3, 161–163

Buck fever, 169

Buckmasters (television show), 81

Business cycles and seasons, 120–122

Business model: changing your, 155–156; existing, surveying your, 160; pivoting to a new, 11, 196; thoroughly knowing your own, 152–153, 180; viewing, perspective for, 153; vulnerabilities in your, questions for scouting out, 154–155

Buying season, 122

Buzzwords, looking beyond, 160

C

Cadillac, 161, 162–163

Camouflage: hiding behind, 51, 53, 63; masters of, 53; shedding the, 51, 57–58, 91–93

Capabilities. *See* Skills and capabilities

Celebration, 178, 179, 180, 181

Challenges: scouting the, 36; taking on, prepared for, 53; understanding, 183; visualization of, 39, 40

Change: executing step-by-step, 156; expecting, 180; incremental, 155–156; inevitability of, 60, 62; radical, using a series of pivots for, 155; rapid pace of, 144

Chevrolet, 161–162

Choices: about focus, thoughts for guiding, 195; and actions, keeping, in alignment, 193; and repercussions, visualizing, 41

Circumstance, flow of, 2

Clarity: about performance patterns, gaining, 106; absolute, benefits of having, 2; and authenticity, 6, 52, 66, 67, 85, 91, 93; of consciousness, 6, 17, 25, 27; lack of, 5, 23, 29, 72; looking at yourself and life with, 102; maintaining, 123; master of, 30–33; as the root of leverage, 103–104; shift from confusion to, 101; in visualization, 41,

171, 175, 176, 181. *See also* Consciousness

Clean exit, finding a, 166, 167

Clean wake, leaving a, 198–200

Closed mindedness, result of, 158

Closers, positioning of, 174–175

Closing with command, 147, 168–177, 181

Clover Technologies, 132–134

Collaboration, productive, laying the groundwork for, 54

Commitment: of allies, confidence in, 78; to consciousness, 48; to giving as much as getting, 77; to a legacy, 8; to obtaining desired endpoint, 30; showing, 69; true, for authentic alliances, 84; to winning, relentless, 11

Commitments, standing by, 78

Common ground, focusing on, 118

Communication: for building/ maintaining alliances, 77, 78, 85–86; for ending alliances, 89–90; and handling tough conversations, 70, 85–86, 89, 94; for presenting Desired Outcomes, 69–70, 86; requirements for authenticity of, 91, 93

Competition, scouting the, 35, 36, 150

Competitors: entry of, building a barrier to prevent, 153, 180; shield from, 81

Confidence, 7, 52, 60, 62, 63, 64, 78, 163, 194

Confusion, 54, 68, 101, 193

Consciousness: alignment resulting from, 193; aspects of, described, 15–48; and being present, 22–25, 181; commitment to, 48; continuing to use, as leverage, 130–131; embedding your vision in your, 175; and ending alliances, 89, 90; essence of, 47; and gaining an elevated viewpoint, 17, 18–22, 74, 85, 102, 153; getting better at building, benefit of, 178; Gilbert as a master of clarity and, 30–33; and intuition, 126; key ideas about, 49–50; and maintaining alliances, 85; major obstacle to, 22–24; in message delivery, 70; of navigators, 15–16; overcoming negativity through, 26–27; overview of, 6; practicing, exercises for, 20, 24–25; process of shifting to, 24–25;

Redford's approach to, 46–47, 48; resulting in real-time execution, 186; and scouting, 33–38; and seeing everything, 38–45; and sighting the target, 27–30; state of, defining the, 17–18; staying in, takeaway on, 94; taking over, awareness of, 10–11; and tracking peak activity periods, 107–108; and understanding your nature, 102; zone of, during the closing, 171

Contacts, layers of, by tier, 135–136

Controllability, uncovering, using visualization for, 43

Conversations. *See* Communication

Costa, Gabe, 202n7

Courage, 165

Credibility, 71

Csikszentmihalyi, Mihaly, 203n1(chap.5)

Cuba trip, 187–188

Culture: of innovation, promoting a, 179; strong, building a, 200

Cycles and seasons: business, 120–122; natural, 104–106, 107, 142, 197–198, 200; reality of, 199

D

Data: arming intuition with, 125, 126; from careful groundwork, 123; interpretation of, 186; necessary, for real-time execution, 148–151, 160, 180; using, 115. *See also* Observation-based strategy

Death, life and, cycle of, 198

Decision making: aligning, 185; authentic, 84; on pivoting, guidelines for, 165–166, 181; training for, 176

Defensiveness, 71, 118

Denial, 74

Desired Outcomes (DO): achieving complete clarity about, 130–131, 171, 176; alignment with, 185; as common ground, 118; describing your, specifically, 67–68; focus on, 24, 25, 30, 65, 118; identifying, 27–30, 31, 32, 66–67, 89, 148, 190; lack of clarity on, 23, 29, 72; laying out your, 66, 68, 80, 90, 94; list of, 109, 139; owning your, 8; potential impacts of players on achieving, seeing, 40–41; presenting, approaches to, 69–70, 86, 138; problems in pursuing, causes of, dealing with, 72–75; process allowing you to achieve, 185–186; pull toward versus push through to, 188; realigning or adapting, 37, 42, 70; revisiting, clarity in, 171, 181; solid, measures of, 29, 68; starting with clearly defined, 119, 190; staying on track to achieving, 30, 38, 111, 116–117, 131, 144, 169; takeaways on, 49, 94, 180, 181; targeted, 2, 7, 30, 75, 85, 150; targeting every action toward, 123; testing steps to change and every pivot against, 156; visualization of, 20, 29, 171–175, 176, 177; on way to achieving, 52; writing down, 176–177; wrong, aiming at, dealing with, 73–74

Details: paying attention to, 38, 174–175; scouting for, 36–37; visualizing, of the entire hunt, 39

Detroit Venture Partners, 179

Differences, looking beyond, 118

Direct Source, getting to the, approach to, 135–136

Discipline, 113

Disciplined Dreaming (Linkner), 179

Disruptions, marketplace, 152, 160

Distractions: avoiding, 17, 37; world of, 53

Diving in, problem with, 18–19

Drift tests, 195–196, 197

Drug addiction analogy, 26

E

Early information, scouting for, 35, 50

Early pivoting, benefits of, 166–167, 181

Early season, 120–121

e-Books, 148

Ecosystem, identifying every element in your, 130, 142

Effort. *See* Energy

Ego: and alignment with life, 190; allowing, to override wisdom, 123; anticipating responses driven by, 40; blinded by, 19, 80, 139; caught in the traps of, 18; disregarding the, 4, 6, 10, 17, 21, 22, 24, 49, 140, 199; facing and understanding your, 89–90; free from, 55, 74, 86, 118, 119, 160–161, 186; helping to subordinate the, means of, 29–30; lies and, 71; listening to our, 23, 24, 48;

networking failures due to, 134; replacing, with authenticity, 193; searching for and destroying any elements of, 68; takeaway on, 94; targets tangled up in, 27–28; time-wasters born in, 111

Elevated viewpoint, gaining an, 17, 18–22, 49, 74, 85, 102, 153

Emotion: allowing, to override wisdom, 123; without, 74, 84, 85, 89, 153, 156

Emotions, negative. *See* Negativity

Energy: aiming your, 51; alignment of, 200; generating, 185; guarding your time and, 109–113, 142; redirecting, 118; running out of, risk of, 197; thoughts for guiding choices about spending, 195; wasting, 71, 139, 188

Entertainment Book, 147

Envy, 111

Evidence-based strategy, 123

Evolution: allowing for, 70; flow of, 2

Excuses: Judge's self-talk becoming, 23; not making, 64–65, 89

Execution: beginning, with a strategy in place, 131;

learning, 4. *See also* Real-time execution

Exit strategy, having an, 166, 167

Experience: decision to pivot or wait based on, 165; of failure, turning around the, 11; flow of, 2; intuition and, 125; learning from, 190; using past, 11, 101, 123, 128

Experiments, considering failures as, 179

F

Facebook, 147

Failure: experience of, turning around the, 11; reframing, 179; self-talk becoming an excuse for, 23

Faith, 148, 183–184, 187

Fake relationships, attempting to leverage, 77

False alarms, avoiding distraction from, 17

False image, maintaining a, 111

False modesty, 92

Farbman Group, 157

Fear, 12, 18, 19, 22, 23, 24, 25, 40, 49, 55, 71, 84, 92, 93, 111, 125, 140

Fearlessness. *See* Confidence

Feedback, 77

Field and Stream (magazine), 145

Fierce conversations. *See* Tough conversations

5-Hour Energy, 159

Flexibility, 42, 70, 138, 144, 166, 190. *See also* Adaptability

Flow: achieving, 178; and alignment, 8, 185, 188–197, 200; ancient roots of, 185; bucking the, 189; building momentum within, 2, 184; connections in, noticing, 35; constant, that surrounds us, 2; defined, 184; finding, 184–185, 194; getting in, 185–188; and knowing about life's cycles, 198; and leaving a clean wake, 198–200; overview of, 8; push toward, 97; recommended reading on, 203n1(chap.5)

Focus: in closing, 172; direct, 51; in execution, 7, 144, 148, 172, 175; having, 2, 17, 19; losing, 30, 92, 151, 169, 176; maintaining, 30, 60, 65, 194; on outcomes, 21, 23, 24, 25, 30, 65, 118; readiness to close with, 187; scouting demanding, 36; on solutions and taking action, 74–75; source of, 4; takeaways on, 49; thoughts

for guiding choices about, 195; visualization enabling, 39, 41, 42, 44, 45, 175, 176

Ford, Henry, 40, 201n2(chap.1)

Freedom, 25, 55, 58, 71, 78

G

Game-changer moments: achieving, example of, 65; uncovering, using visualization for, 43

Game-playing environment: avoiding a, benefits of, 54; behavior in a, 53

Gatekeepers, getting to the, 134–139, 142

Gates, Bill, 56

General Motors (GM), 64–65, 67, 146, 161, 162

Gilbert, Dan, 3, 30–33, 43, 76, 103, 104

Globalization, effect of, 129

GNC, 159

Goals: fluidity of, 29, 171; identifying, questions for, 28–29, 190–193. *See also* Desired Outcomes (DO); Ultimate goals

Gossiping, 109, 111

Greed, 51, 111

Groundwork: careful, data from, 123; doing the, 37, 90, 136, 163; essential, best time for taking care of, 120; laying the, 54; some, time for doing, 122

Groupon, 147

Guilt, 84, 110

Gut reactions, 60, 126, 128

H

Happiness, 4, 30, 53, 193

Herding mentality, 95

Hero role, 75

Honesty, 51, 53, 54, 66, 67, 70, 77, 79, 84, 89, 199. *See also* Authenticity

Hunt, The: beginning, at an early age, 3–4; benefits of, and results of straying from the core principles, 5; elements of, overview of, 5–8; experience of, 185; foundation for, formation of the, 9–11; guarantee of the, 8–9; most fundamental skill of, 17; as a process, 179; reason for the success of, 11–12; relevancy of, 5; tactics of, 2; training for, 140; who can benefit from, 13–14. *See also* Authenticity; Consciousness; Flow; Leverage; Real-time execution

Hunter's Vision, seeing everything with, 39–45, 50

Hunter's Wisdom, 142; allowing emotion or ego to override, 123; exercising, 97; leveraging, 113–116, 119

I

Ignorance, cost of, 18

Illusions, 102

Imagining. *See* Visualization

Inc. (magazine), 133

Indecision, 84

Innovation: culture of, promoting a, 179; engines of, 4–5; flow of, 2; tweaks and, 147; unleashed, laying the groundwork for, 54

Insecurity, 12, 22, 55, 90

Instincts. *See* Natural instincts

Interaction: flow of, 2; watching different types of, 157

Intuition, 114, 115–116, 123, 125–128, 165. *See also* Natural instincts

iTunes, 152

J

Jenkinson, William, 202n7

Jeremiah Johnson (movie), 46

Jobs, Steve, 56

Jordan, Bill, 58, 76

Journey, success coming from the, 175–176, 200

Judge: control held by the, 23, 24; flipping from, to Scout, 25; maintaining strong

relationships and the, 84;
observing as the, avoiding, 6;
seeing other perspectives and
the, 118; silencing the, 26–27,
49; voice of the, 22–23

K

Knee-jerk reactions, 84
Knowing, 186–187, 198. *See also*
Consciousness
Knowledge, decision to pivot or
wait based on, 165

L

Landscape, scouting the, 35–36
LaNeve, Mark, 162
Leadership gaps, looking for, 43
Leadership shift, 196
Leapfrogging, 153
Learning: from all types of
experiences, 190; from
breakthrough and breakout
moments, 178; for future
use, 171; from mistakes, 9,
19, 41; from nature, biggest
lesson to emerge out of, 198;
remaining open to, 38, 47;
from someone else's mistakes
and successes, 140; from the
WHA experience, 9–11, 19,
41, 69, 95–96, 144–145, 190
Led Zeppelin campaign,
162–163

Legacy: commitment to a, 8;
leaving a clean wake as your,
198–200
Leverage: alignment resulting from, 194; aspects of,
described, 95–141; attempting with fake relationships,
77; benefiting from, 33;
benefits of, 97–98; critical
skills of, 97; devising tweaks
as, 159; getting better at
building, benefit of, 178; and
getting to the gatekeepers,
134–139; and guarding your
time and energy, 109–113;
human capabilities used as,
184; Hunter's Wisdom and,
113–116; information pro-
viding, 25; key ideas about,
141–142; and oneness with
others, 115, 116–119; overview of, 7; of past successes,
198; power of, 95; resulting in
real-time execution, 186; root
of all, 103–104; Schiefelbein's
use of, 132–134; sharing, with
others, 132, 139; tiered, 135–
136, 138, 142; and tightening
your strategy, 116, 119–124;
timing of, 139; and tracking
your natural cycle and season,
104–109; and understand-
ing your nature, 98–102,

111–112, 113; using, 2, 7, 11, 62, 93, 95, 97, 146, 148, 153, 163, 175; wanting to, for all it's worth, 200; and willing the win, 116, 125–128; working at building and practicing, 139–141; yourself as a source of, 132, 141

Leverage Jet Stream: building a, 128–132, 142; and getting to the gatekeepers, 137–138; riding on the, example of, 132–134; starting your own, by learning from others, 140

Leverage log, 124–125

Leverage points: access to, 139; defined, 128; finding, authenticity helping with, 131; lies weakening, 71; looking for, 96; mapping, 131; tracking, 124; unique, finding your own, 160; using, 128

Lies: avoiding, importance of, 54; most dangerous, 91–92; telling, to oneself, 101; truths about, 71

Life: alignment with, 188–197; approach to, 184–185; cycle of, 198, 200; natural order of, 198; opportunity created by, 2, 194; showing up in, 49

"Like a Rock" campaign, 162

Limits, setting, 112

Linkner, Josh, 76, 179

Listening, 17, 46–47, 60, 86, 90, 126, 139, 142, 157

Lone-wolf approach, 95

Long-range goals. *See* Ultimate goals

Long-term vision, having, 38

Losing, fear of, 55

Loyalty, 84

Luck, 14, 15, 119, 125, 132

M

Macro clarity, seeing with, 41

Macro data, 149, 150, 180

Macro-Scouting, 35–36, 50

Manning, Peyton, 144

Markers, 177–180

Marketplace disruptions, 152, 160

Marking the target, 63–70

McDonald's, 154

Meaning, of goals, thinking about, 191–192, 195

Meditation, 144

Meditation tool, 45, 173

Michael Waddell's Bone Collector (television show), 58, 83

Micro data, 149–150, 180

Micro focus, enabling, 41

Micro-Scouting, 36–37, 50

Microsoft, 56

Milestones, marking, 177–180

Mistakes: failing to take responsibility for, 78; learning from, 9, 19, 41; learning from someone else's, 140; owning your, 75; source of, 5

Momentum, 2, 177, 184, 185, 188, 194, 198

Motives: alignment with, 185; assessing your, 89–90; being honest about, 6; faith in, 184

Mundt, Nick, 81–82

MySpace, 147

N

NASCAR, 161

Native territory: claiming new territory as your, example of, 62–63; claiming your, 59–62; standing in your, 80; takeaways on, 93

Natural cycles and seasons, 104–106, 107, 142, 197–198, 199

Natural instincts: animals exploiting their, 54, 96; awakening your, 193; as hunters, 1, 97; and inherent nature, 125; leveraging our, need for, 1–2, 97; primal, pushing our, to the next level, 200; waking up your, 140. *See also* Intuition

Natural order: of life, 198; succeeding within the, faith in and, 183–184

Nature: inherent, 125, 139; shared, 115, 116, 119. *See also* Authentic nature; Unique nature

Navigators, 15–16

Navigator's map, 39

Negativity: avoiding being lured by, 49, 84, 90, 140; driven by, 111; lies fueling, 92; overcoming, 26–27, 91–93; result of, 187–188. *See also* Judge; *specific negative emotions and thoughts*

Netflix, 152, 153–154

Networking: process of, 134–139; relentless, 141

Networks, building and using, 97, 128–132

Neutrality. *See* Objectivity/neutrality

New territory: claiming, as your native territory, example of, 62–63; claiming your, 153, 161–163; determining whether to move into, 149; strategy for moving into, developing a, 147, 158–161

Niche industries, 129

Nimbleness/agility, 148, 152

O

Objectivity/neutrality, 19, 38, 42, 43, 85, 123. *See also* Consciousness

Observation: benefit of, 4; clarity for, 17; flow of, 2; intuition and, 125; neutrality of, 85; as True Hunters, 6. *See also* Scouting

Observation-based strategy, 115, 116, 119–124, 142

Obstacles: fluidly moving around, 189; major, to consciousness, 22–24. *See also* Ego; Negativity

Off-season, 120

Oneness with your prey/others, 115, 116–119

Openers, positioning of, 174

Openness, 38, 47

Opportunists, 7, 96, 97

Opportunities: available, getting smarter about, 36; hidden, 60; identifying and leveraging, 2, 7, 11, 96, 97, 98, 141; missing, 48; new, confidence to go after, 62, 63; nonstop, leveraging, 184; real-time, guided by, 148; recognizing, 147–148; source of, 2, 194; for spotting targets, 120; taking on, prepared for, 53; understanding, 183; visualizing, 39, 40, 42–43. *See also* Leverage

Outcomes: bigger and better, on track towards, 8; focus on, 21, 23, 25; original, getting back on the trail of, 10–11;

owning your, 65, 72–75, 94; successful, visualization of, 40; undefined, 27. *See also* Desired Outcomes (DO)

Outdoor Channel, 58, 83

Outdoor Life (magazine), 145

OutdoorHub (OHub), 11, 99, 100, 101, 137–138, 145–146, 150, 155, 157, 196–197

P

Packs, hunting in, value of, 75–76. *See also* Alliances

Paro, Jeff, 83

Passion, 10, 30, 54, 69, 106

Path, choosing your, 155–156

Patience, 4, 165, 189

Peak activity window (PAW): identifying and leveraging, 142; identifying and leveraging your, 105–109; protecting your, 112, 142; tool for calculating, 202n1

Performance patterns: tracking, 124; understanding, 105–106, 107, 108–109, 142

Personal brand: establishing and expressing your, 56–58, 62, 93; exercise for thinking about your, 61

Perspectives: gaining other, 47, 48; multiple, building, 39; seeing other, 40, 42, 44, 50, 89, 118

Pitfalls: scouting the, 36; visualization of, 39

Pivotal indicators, spotting, 43

Pivoting: allowing, when necessary, 127, 131; being present for, 156–158; better position for, 42; deciding between waiting or, 165–166, 181; early, benefits of, 166–167, 181; to a new business model, 11, 196; on-the-fly, 144, 145, 146, 147, 148, 151–156; takeaways on, 180, 181

Pivots, testing, against your Desired Outcomes, 156

Players: scouting the, 35, 36, 149; seeing the, and the relationships involved, 40–41; visualizing challenges faced by you and, 39

Poker game analogy, 53

Posing, 77

Position: better, for pivoting, 42; holding your, 168, 170; to start tracking, 23

Possibilities: leaving a wake of, 186; range of, opening your mind to a, 44. *See also* Opportunities

Postseason, 122

Potential success, pulling in more, 186

Power source, 129, 183–184, 197

Pre-buying season, 121

Predatory wisdom. *See* Hunter's Wisdom

Preparation, importance of, 112

Pre-Season Scouting, 35

Pride, 90

Primal triggers/activities, 115, 116. *See also* Natural instincts

Proactive, being, importance of, 154

Problems and issues: getting to the root of, for clarity, 28, 31–32; in pursuing Desired Outcomes, causes of, dealing with, 72–75; questions for understanding, 74; seeing, through each other's eyes, 118

Procrastinating, 110

Pull versus push, 188

Purpose, of goals, thinking about, 192, 195

Q

Quicken Loans, 3, 30–31, 33, 103

R

Radar scan, 34, 157

Real estate business, 126

Realignment, 37, 196–197

Reality: being blind to, 80; of cycles, 199; grounded in, importance of, 51, 81; guided by, 19, 21, 26; hard-core, 123; losing track of, 24; negative, making a, 26, 49; that you want to live in, 93; wisdom based on, 127. *See also* Authenticity; Consciousness

Real-time execution: alignment resulting from, 194, 197; aspects of, described, 143–180; benefits of, 143, 147–148; Brink's illustration of, 161–163; and claiming your territory, 161–163; and closing with command, 168–177, 168–177; defined, 143; elements critical to, 146–147; fluidity of, 172, 175; getting better at achieving, means of, 178; important markers in, 177–180; key ideas about, 180–181; and knowing when to stick it out and when to walk away, 147, 163–167; master of, 144; moving into new territory in, developing strategies for, 147, 158–161; overview of, 7–8; pivoting in, 144, 145, 146, 147, 148, 151–158; processes resulting in, 186; requirements for, 148; sustaining, means of, 177; targeting and tracking in, 146, 148–151, 159–160; at work, 144–146

Realtree (company), 76

Realtree Outdoors (television show), 58, 81, 82

Redford, Robert, 46–47, 48

Reflection, 85, 153

Reflexive response, natural, 7, 33

Relationships: building, 55, 83, 157; defined by authenticity, 77–78; establishing authentic, 79–80; fake, attempting to leverage, 77; investing in, takeaway on, 94; lies weakening, 71; strong, action that maintains, 84; trust-based, 53; visualizing the players and, 79–80. *See also* Alliances

Respect, 66, 85, 87, 89, 109

Responsibility, taking, 77, 78, 94, 199

Revenge, need for, 90

Review: daily, 124; season to regroup and, 122

Revolution, flow of, 2

Rhythm, living in, 188. *See also* Flow

Risks: calculating, 60, 62, 63; investment, 76; keeping

informed of, 53; in not being
agile, 152; of running out of
time and energy, 197; timely
and well-calculated, 72
Rock Gaming, 31
Roles, 75, 175, 183
Ruth, Babe, 64, 202n7

S
Sadness, 49
Safeguards, 195–196
Schiefelbein, Jim, 132–134
Scott, Susan, 85, 202n8
Scout: being present as the, 22,
25–26; benefits from being a,
34; flipping from Judge to, 25;
maintaining strong relationships as the, 84; observing
as the, 6, 20; tracking peak
activity periods as the,
107–108, 142
Scouting: for data, 149–150;
necessary, for ending alliances,
90; a new path, 144–145;
ongoing, 153; out vulnerabilities, questions for, 154–155;
role of, in consciousness,
33–38; seasonal approach to,
120, 121, 122; takeaways on,
50; time spent, 110; types of,
35–37
Seasons. *See* Cycles and seasons

Senses, tapping into your, 45
Shame, 18, 90, 164
Short-term goals, drivers of, 190.
See also Desired Outcomes
(DO)
"Should be" illusions, 102
Shutting up, 75, 138–139,
142
Sighting the target, 27–30
Silence, 168, 170
Size, of goals, thinking about,
192–193
Skills and capabilities: alignment
with, 185; believing in your,
92; confidence in, of allies, 78;
leveraging, 62, 184; staying
honest about, 53; testing and
growing your, 60
Sloppiness, 37
Small Business Administration,
133
Solutions: finding, moving for-
ward after, 28, 31–32; focused
on finding, and taking action,
74–75
Spirituality, 183–184
Stalling, 110
Staples, 133
Stealth, 4, 36, 37, 50, 53, 158
Stewardship, 199
Strategic choices, considering
potential consequences of, 41

Strategy: exit, having an, 166, 167; learning, 4; losing, sticking too long with a, result of, 166; for moving into new territory, developing a, 147, 158–161; observation-based, 115, 116, 119–124; for presenting Desired Outcomes, having a, importance of, 69–70; pulling together your own, data for, 150; seasonal approach to, 120–122; seeing the tactical steps for waging your, 42–43; for setting your Leverage Jet Stream in motion, 129, 130–131

Strengths: building, 77; connecting data to current, 160; identifying existing product, 159; leveraging, 62, 93, 98, 141; owning your, 51, 54; playing to your, 61; pooling, 78; testing and growing your, 60; understanding your, 54, 98

Success: elements for, availability of, 2; meaning of, 175–176, 200; potential, pulling in more, 186; someone else's, learning from, 140

Sundance Institute, 46

Suspicion, handling, 79–80

T

Talent, leveraging, 175

Targeting: benefit of, 4; every action, 123; lack of clarity in, 23, 29; ongoing, 153; in real-time execution, 7, 146, 148–151, 159–160, 180; visualization of, 20

Targets: bull's-eye of, hitting, precision and clarity for, 41; having absolute clarity about, 52; lack of clear, 5; marking your, 63–70; missing, 27; outcomes that form, 29; recalibrating approach to, reasons for, 72; sighting your, 27–30; spotting, opportunities for, 120; tangled up, 27–28; unnecessary missed, avoiding, 66. *See also* Desired outcomes (DO)

Teams. *See* Alliances

Technological advancements, effect of, 129

Template, creating a, 175

Territory: elements for success in our, 2; same, hunting the, 200; taking command of any, examples of, 3, 11; understanding of the, 15, 16, 17; unscouted, 19. *See also* Native territory; New territory; Scouting

Thoughts, negative. *See*
Negativity
Tiered leverage, 135–136, 138,
142
Time: guarding your, 109–113,
142; investment of, in building
alliances, 76; to pivot, knowing
the, elements in, 153–155; to
regroup and review, 122; running out of, risk of, 197; saving,
66; for taking care of essential
groundwork, 120; thoughts for
guiding choices about spending, 195; wasting, 71, 77, 109,
110–111, 112, 139, 188
Time-outs, 24
Timing, 139
Tough conversations, 70, 85–86,
89, 94
Towbes, Michael, 165
Tracking: benefit of, 4; essential
tool for, 35; ongoing, 153;
of peak activity periods,
104–109, 142; position to
start, 23; in real-time
execution, 146, 148–151,
159–160, 180; staying on
track while, 60
Training, 6, 7, 21, 40–42, 51,
101, 140, 147, 176. *See also*
Weight-training
Transition, fluid, allowing for
a, 167

Transparency, 91
Traps. *See* Ego; Fear
Trends: knowing the, 149; scouting for, 35, 36; staying ahead
of, 180–181
Trigger-happy behavior, avoiding, 18–19, 49
Trophies: outcomes that form,
29; taking, key to, 98; walking
away without, 87. *See also*
Desired Outcomes (DO)
True Hunters: benefits from
being, 4–5, 12–13; defined,
13; examples of, 3; honing
abilities to become, 4; spiritual
basis of, 183–184; successful,
way of, 2; who can ben-
efit from being, 14. *See also*
Authenticity; Consciousness;
Flow; Leverage; Real-time
execution
Trust, 53, 76, 77, 127, 128, 148
Truthfulness. *See* Honesty
Turner, Travis "T-Bone,"
41, 82
Tweaks, 147, 156, 159,
175, 197

U
Ultimate goals: alignment of,
185, 193–194; identifying,
190–193; as safeguards,
195–196

Unique nature: exploiting your, 97; owning your, 102; seeing someone else's, 118; understanding and leveraging your, 98–102, 111–112, 113, 141. *See also* Authentic nature

V

VA (Void Analysis) programs, 126

Valpak, 147

Variables, covering, 93, 119, 175, 187

Vetting strategies, 123

Victim role, 75, 101

Viewpoint, elevated, gaining an, 17, 18–22, 49, 74, 85, 102, 153

Villain role, 75

Virgin Group, 62, 63, 202n6

Vision: confidence in your, 163; embedding your, in your consciousness, 175; long-term, having, 38; new, following a, approach to, 199–200; unemotional, 153, 156

Visualization: of the closing moments, 171–175, 176, 177, 181; of how actions will play out, 183; hunter's embracing, 39, 201n1(chap.1);

leveraging, 125, 129; power of, 44; role of, in consciousness, 20, 21, 29, 38–44; takeaways on, 50, 181; tool for, using a, 45, 173; as training the mind, 40–42, 176

Vulnerabilities. *See* Weaknesses

W

Waddell, Michael, 58–59, 82, 169. *See also* Bone Collector Brotherhood

Waiting, deciding between pivoting or, 165–166, 181

"Walk the talk," 57, 59

Walmart, 159

Weaknesses: exposing your, 78; in the final stretch, 169; identifying areas of, 153; identifying existing product, 159; leveraging, 98, 141; minimizing, 77, 93; other people's, uncovering, 42–43; owning your, 51, 54; playing to your, 61; scouting out, questions for, 154–155; in strategy, uncovering, 123; understanding your, 54, 141

Weight-training, 7, 77, 140

Wendy's, 154

Whisner, Mac, 161–162

Wild Kingdom (television show),
   122
Willing the win, 116, 125–128
Winning on your own terms,
   53–54, 55
Wisdom: allowing emotion to
   override, 123; conventional/
   common, 13, 102; open to,
   126–127. *See also* Hunter's
   Wisdom

World Hunting Association
   (WHA), experience of, learning from the, 9–11, 19, 41, 69,
   95–96, 144–145, 190
World stewardship, 199

Y
YouTube, 99, 100

Z
Zen-like control, 170